THE AUSTRALIAN
Women's Weekly
slow cooker 3
fuss-free meals — minimal cooking with maximum flavour

MEDIA GROUP

CONTENTS

The oven temperatures in this book are for conventional ovens; if you have a fan-forced oven, decrease the temperature by 10-20 degrees. A measurement conversion chart appears on the back flap of this book.

Take it slowly	4
Poultry	8
Beef & Veal	24
Lamb	44
Pork	64
Vegetables	80
Puddings	100
Stocks	110
Cooking Techniques	112
Glossary	114
Index	117

TAKE IT SLOWLY

As the days grow shorter, there's nothing quite as comforting as the delicious aroma of a slow-cooked meal. There's something deeply satisfying about a hearty meal that rewards you with rich flavours, tender meat and soft vegetables.

Food tastes all the better when it takes only a little preparation, and slow cooking is a proven success because of the ease it affords busy home cooks. Slow cookers are ideal as the meal practically cooks itself.

Slow cookers are available in a wide range of shapes and sizes. We used the most popular-sized slow cooker, a 4.5-litre (18-cup) slow cooker to test all our recipes. If you have a smaller or larger cooker, don't panic, simply reduce or increase the amount of liquid and quantity of food.

All slow cookers are different and come with a variety of bells and whistles, so the first step before turning it on is to read the manufacturer's instructions. This includes reading important safety measures, such as not leaving the appliance unattended at any time, or touching any of the metal parts while the cooker is in use. It will also outline the settings for operating the slow cooker. For example, some slow cookers have a 'warm' setting. This setting does not cook your food; instead it is designed to maintain the food's temperature until you are ready to eat. We suggest that if you are happy to leave the slow cooker on all day then use the low setting or, if you're in a bit more of a hurry, cut the cooking time in half by turning the slow cooker up to the high setting.

Remember, as tempting as it is to lift the lid of the slow cooker, your dish will cook better if you don't. Each time you lift the lid, heat escapes, which can set your cooking time back by up to half an hour.

THE BEST CUTS TO USE

Extended cooking times makes slow cooking budget-friendly, and perfect for feeding large crowds. Cheaper, tougher cuts of red meat are perfect for the slow cooker – so why waste more expensive cuts?

BEEF We suggest using topside, chuck, oyster, blade and round steak for slow cooking.

LAMB Use neck chops, shanks, and boneless shoulder. The long, slow cooking time will transform these secondary cuts into tender, flavoursome meat.

PORK The best cuts include forequarter chops, neck, shoulder and belly.

POULTRY All kinds of poultry (chicken, turkey, etc) work well in a slow cooker, but pieces on the bone, such as drumsticks or marylands, work best. The most important thing to remember when using poultry is to avoid overcooking it; overcooking will make it dry and stringy.

OTHER MEATS Other types of stewing meats, such as venison, goat, kangaroo, hare and rabbit, are also great for slow cooking.

SEAFOOD Generally, seafood is not suitable for use in the slow cooker as it toughens quickly. However, large octopus is fine as the slow cooker tenderises the meat.

You can also use the slow cooker to cook a great variety of sauces and soups that work brilliantly with seafood, such as prawns and mussels, which can be added just before you serve.

GETTING THE LIQUID CONTENT RIGHT

SOUP This is the easiest dish to make in the slow cooker; just ensure the cooker is at least half full before you start.

ROASTS These are normally cooked with minimal liquid in a slow cooker, especially if the meat is placed on top of the vegetables. You can add a small amount of liquid if you wish to make a sauce or gravy.

CASSEROLES, STEWS, CURRIES AND TAGINES As a general rule of thumb, the slow cooker should be at least half full when cooking any of these tasty dishes. For the best results place the vegetables into the cooker first, then the meat, and finally add the liquid.

CORNED MEATS Cook these meats using enough liquid to barely cover them. This will result in a delicious meal.

THE TRICK FOR FLAVOURSOME MEAT

While slow cookers are all about simply throwing your ingredients in and letting the cooker do the work, if you take a few moments to brown the meat you will enhance both the flavour and colour of the ingredients. Using a large, heated and oiled frying pan, add the meat in small batches, turning every so often to ensure that it browns evenly. Make sure the pan is on a medium-high heat and there is a sufficient amount of oil before adding the meat, otherwise it will stew instead of caramelise. And, the best thing is, by doing it this way, is that you can brown the meat the night before, and slow cook it the next day. Simply pop it in an airtight container, along with any juices from the meat, and refrigerate it until the next day.

THE FACTS ON FAT

Slow cooking meat often results in a lot of fat being extracted. The best way to remove the excess fat is to refrigerate the cooked food, as the fat will then sit on the top of the pan juices and can then be easily lifted off.

If you are looking to serve the meal straightaway, don't stress; one of the easiest ways to remove fat is to soak it up with absorbent paper towel or a shallow spoon. Wait for about half an hour to let the dish settle and the fat rise, then carefully dip the paper towel in to soak up the visible fat.

There are a couple of great kitchen gadgets you can buy from cookware shops to help remove the fat. We recommend either a special kind of 'brush' that simply sweeps away the fat, or there is a 'jug' available that separates the fat from the pan juices (the spout is at the base

of the jug, below the level of the fat, so when the jug is tipped over, the pan juices, not the fat, is poured out).

FREEZING LEFTOVERS
Due to the large volume of food it is possible to produce using slow cookers, you may end up with leftovers. The best thing to do is to freeze them so you can conveniently enjoy the dish another time. There is a large amount of liquid in a slow cooker, so the best way to freeze the meal is to place the vegetables and meat into freezer-friendly containers, then pour in the liquid until it just covers the food. Be sure to write the date that the dish was cooked on the container, as it is only suitable to be stored for up to three months. Each recipe has notes on whether or not it is suitable to freeze.

A LITTLE WORD ON DRIED BEANS
Certain dry beans need to be cooked before being added to the slow cooker because of a particular chemical they contain. Kidney-shaped beans of all colours and sizes are related to each other and must be washed, drained and boiled in fresh water until tender before adding to the slow-cooker. Once they are cooked, they can be safely added to the slow cooker, just like canned beans.

It is fine to use chickpeas and soya beans raw; just rinse them well before use.

CLEANING
The slow cooker insert can be washed in hot soapy water. Soak the insert in warm water and scrub using a plastic or nylon brush to help remove cooked-on food. Do not use scourers or chemicals to clean the cooker as they can damage the surface. Read the instruction manual first, but most slow cooker inserts are dishwasher-proof.
To clean the outside of the slow cooker, simply wipe down with a damp cloth and dry.

POULTRY

chicken hot and sour soup

PREP + COOK TIME 9 HOURS **SERVES** 6

1.6kg (3¼-pound) whole chicken

2 medium carrots (240g), chopped coarsely

2 stalks celery (300g), trimmed, chopped coarsely

1 large brown onion (200g), chopped coarsely

2.5-litres (10-cups) water

6 fresh kaffir lime leaves, crushed

2 x 10cm (4-inch) stalks lemon grass, bruised

6cm (2½-inch) piece fresh ginger (30g), grated

2 fresh long red chillies, sliced thinly

½ cup (125ml) lime juice

½ cup (125ml) fish sauce

3 teaspoons brown sugar

425g (13½ ounces) canned straw mushrooms, rinsed, drained

2 baby buk choy (300g), trimmed, chopped coarsely

200g (6½ ounces) rice vermicelli noodles

½ cup firmly packed fresh coriander leaves (cilantro)

1 Remove and discard fat and skin from the chicken. Place chicken, carrot, celery, onion and the water in a 4.5-litre (18-cup) slow cooker. Cook, covered, on low, for 8 hours.

2 Carefully remove chicken from cooker; shred the meat coarsely using two forks. Discard bones. Strain cooking liquid through a muslin-lined sieve, clean chux or linen tea towel; discard solids.

3 Return strained liquid to cooker with lime leaves, lemon grass, ginger, chilli, juice, sauce, sugar, mushrooms and chicken. Cook, covered, on high for 30 minutes. Stir in buk choy.

4 Meanwhile, place noodles in a medium heatproof bowl, cover with boiling water; stand 10 minutes or until softened, drain. Divide noodles among serving bowls. Ladle hot soup over noodles. Serve sprinkled with coriander, and fresh sliced chilli, if you like.

Suitable to freeze at the end of step 3.

nutritional count per serving
- 16.5g total fat
- 5g saturated fat
- 1482kJ (354 cal)
- 13.4g carbohydrate
- 34.5g protein
- 6.2g fibre

POULTRY

portuguese turkey

PREP + COOK TIME 6½ HOURS SERVES 6

27 cloves garlic, peeled
¼ cup (30g) sea salt flakes
2 teaspoons sweet paprika
2 tablespoons duck fat
3 turkey drumsticks (2.5kg)
2 cups (500ml) tawny port
½ cup (125ml) dry white wine

1 Blend or process garlic, salt and paprika in a food processor until smooth. Transfer to a small bowl. Stir in duck fat; it will be solid at first, but will soften and combine as it's stirred.
2 Spoon garlic mixture over the turkey legs then, using your hands, rub into the skin.
3 Place turkey legs in a 4.5-litre (18-cup) slow cooker. Add port and wine.

POULTRY

Depending on the size of your cooker, you may need to ask the butcher to chop off the end of each drumstick. This dish is traditionally served at Christmas time.

4 Cook, covered, on low, for 6 hours. Using a spoon or small ladle, skim fat from surface of liquid.
5 Serve meat shredded in large chunks with cooking juices spooned over.

serving suggestion Serve with sautéed potatoes and a bitter greens salad.
tip We used a chardonnay-style wine in this recipe.

Suitable to freeze at the end of step 2.

nutritional count per serving
▸ 38.8g total fat
▸ 12.8g saturated fat
▸ 3028kJ (723 cal)
▸ 12g carbohydrate
▸ 62g protein
▸ 2.3g fibre

POULTRY

Chicken thigh cutlets usually come with the skin and centre bone intact, although sometimes they can be found without the skin. Poultry shops and most major supermarkets will sell them.

honey-mustard chicken

PREP + COOK TIME 6¾ HOURS   SERVES 4

2 tablespoons cornflour (cornstarch)
2 teaspoons dry mustard powder
½ cup (125ml) dry white wine
1 cup (250ml) chicken stock
¼ cup (70g) wholegrain mustard
2 tablespoons honey
8 chicken thigh cutlets (1.6kg)
1 medium leek (350g), trimmed, sliced thickly
2 stalks celery (300g), trimmed, sliced thickly
400g (12½ ounces) baby carrots, peeled
1 cup (120g) frozen peas
⅓ cup (80ml) pouring cream
¼ cup coarsely chopped fresh flat-leaf parsley

1 Place cornflour and mustard powder in a 4.5-litre (18-cup) slow cooker. Gradually whisk in wine and stock until smooth. Add mustard and honey; whisk until smooth.
2 Remove and discard fat and skin from chicken. Place chicken, leek, celery and carrots in cooker. Cook, covered, on low, for 6 hours.
3 Add peas to cooker; cook, covered, for 20 minutes. Stir in cream; season to taste. Sprinkle chicken with parsley to serve.

tip We used a chardonnay-style wine in this recipe.

Not suitable to freeze.

nutritional count per serving
- 28.9g total fat
- 10.9g saturated fat
- 2636kJ (630 cal)
- 27.8g carbohydrate
- 58.1g protein
- 9.1g fibre

POULTRY

While in America chicken maryland is a traditional crumbed-chicken dish, in Australia it refers to a cut of chicken consisting of the leg (drumstick) and thigh in one piece with the skin and bone intact. It is available from chicken shops and many larger supermarkets.

apricot chicken

PREP + COOK TIME 6½ HOURS SERVES 6

45g (1½-ounce) packet cream of chicken simmer soup mix

1⅔ cups (410ml) apricot nectar

6 chicken marylands (2.1kg)

1 medium leek (350g), trimmed, sliced thickly

2 cloves garlic, crushed

¾ cup (75g) dried apricot halves

¼ cup coarsely chopped fresh flat-leaf parsley

1 Place the soup mix in a 4.5-litre (18-cup) slow cooker. Gradually whisk in nectar until smooth. Season to taste.
2 Remove and discard fat and skin from the chicken. Place chicken, leek, garlic and apricots in cooker. Cook, covered, on low, for 6 hours.
3 Sprinkle chicken with parsley to serve.

serving suggestion Mashed potato and steamed green beans.

Suitable to freeze at the end of step 2.

nutritional count per serving
▸ 12.1g total fat
▸ 3.7g saturated fat
▸ 1400kJ (334 cal)
▸ 21.3g carbohydrate
▸ 33.8g protein
▸ 2.7g fibre

POULTRY

Garam masala is a blend of spices including cloves, cardamom, cinnamon, coriander, fennel and cumin, that are roasted and ground together. Black pepper and chilli can be added for a hotter version.

chicken mulligatawny

PREP + COOK TIME 8½ HOURS SERVES 4

2 medium brown onions (300g), chopped coarsely
2 cloves garlic, chopped coarsely
2 medium carrots (240g), chopped coarsely
1 stalk celery (150g), trimmed, chopped coarsely
1 fresh long red chilli, chopped coarsely
4cm (1½-inch) piece fresh ginger (20g), grated
2 chicken marylands (700g)
1 tablespoon mild curry powder
1 teaspoon ground cumin
1 teaspoon garam masala
3 cups (750ml) chicken stock
1 cup (250ml) coconut milk
½ cup loosely packed fresh coriander leaves (cilantro)

1 Place onion, garlic, carrot, celery, chilli, ginger, chicken, curry powder, cumin, garam masala and stock in a 4.5-litre (18-cup) slow cooker. Cook, covered, on low, for 8 hours.
2 Carefully remove chicken from the cooker; discard the skin and bones. Shred meat coarsely using two forks.
3 Skim fat from the surface of the vegetable mixture. Blend or process vegetable mixture until smooth. Return chicken to the pan with the coconut milk; stir to combine. Ladle soup into serving bowls; sprinkle with coriander to serve, and drizzle with extra coconut milk, if you like.

Suitable to freeze at the end of step 3.

nutritional count per serving
- 20.4g total fat
- 13.4g saturated fat
- 1437kJ (343 cal)
- 11.1g carbohydrate
- 27g protein
- 5.3g fibre

serving suggestion

To serve, sprinkle with thinly sliced red chillies and green onions, and accompany with peking duck pancakes and hoisin sauce.

POULTRY

Peking duck is Beijing's most famous dish. Peking became known in the West as Beijing after the government of the day applied the Latin alphabet to their language; however, Beijing is still known as Peking by the locals. Traditionally, this dish is served with peking duck pancakes and hoisin sauce.

peking duck

PREP + COOK TIME 6¾ HOURS SERVES 4

8 green onions (scallions), trimmed, halved crossways

2 teaspoons five-spice powder

1 teaspoon ground cinnamon

½ teaspoon ground nutmeg

2 teaspoons sea salt flakes

2 tablespoons honey

1 tablespoon soy sauce

2.1kg (4¼-pound) whole duck

1 medium lemon (140g), sliced thickly

5cm (2-inch) piece fresh ginger (25g), sliced thickly

2 star anise

1 Place onions over the base of a 4.5-litre (18-cup) slow cooker.
2 Combine five-spice, cinnamon, nutmeg, salt, honey and sauce in a small bowl.
3 Remove excess fat from duck cavity, then cut off the neck and discard with the fat. Rub salt mixture over duck. Fill cavity with lemon, ginger and star-anise. Transfer duck to the cooker. Cook, covered, on low, for 6 hours.

Not suitable to freeze.

---

nutritional count per serving
▶ 21.1g total fat
▶ 6.4g saturated fat
▶ 2200kJ (526 cal)
▶ 14.8g carbohydrate
▶ 67.7g protein
▶ 1.6g fibre

sticky balsamic roast chicken

PREP + COOK TIME 6½ HOURS SERVES 4

4 cloves garlic, crushed

½ cup (125ml) balsamic vinegar

2 tablespoons dijon mustard

1 tablespoon brown sugar

1 tablespoon olive oil

2 tablespoons coarsely chopped fresh oregano

2 tablespoons coarsely chopped fresh flat-leaf parsley

2kg (4-pound) whole chicken

1 Place garlic, vinegar, mustard, sugar, oil and half each of the oregano and parsley in a 4.5-litre (18-cup) slow cooker; stir to combine.
2 Discard excess fat from chicken cavity. Place chicken in cooker; turn to coat in mixture. Cook, covered, on low, for 6 hours.
3 Carefully remove chicken from cooker; cover to keep warm. Transfer cooking liquid to a medium frying pan; skim and discard fat from surface of cooking liquid. Bring liquid to the boil. Boil, uncovered, for 10 minutes or until sauce is reduced to ½ cup. Drizzle chicken with the sauce; sprinkle with remaining herbs to serve.

Not suitable to freeze.

nutritional count per serving
▶ 34.7g total fat
▶ 9.8g saturated fat
▶ 2408kJ (575 cal)
▶ 10.1g carbohydrate
▶ 54g protein
▶ 1.3g fibre

serving suggestion
Rocket, and roasted potatoes and truss cherry tomatoes.

turkey with bacon, celery and sage seasoning

PREP + COOK TIME 9½ HOURS SERVES 6

2 medium brown onions (300g)
2.2kg (5-pound) turkey hindquarter
2 teaspoons vegetable oil
60g (2 ounces) butter
1 clove garlic, chopped finely
4 rindless middle-cut bacon slices (175g), chopped finely
1 stalk celery (150g), trimmed, chopped finely
2 cups (140g) stale breadcrumbs
1 egg
1 tablespoon chopped fresh sage
½ cup (125ml) water
2 tablespoons plain (all-purpose) flour
½ cup (160g) cranberry sauce

1 Cut one onion into wedges; place wedges in a 4.5-litre (18-cup) slow cooker. Finely chop remaining onion; reserve.
2 Cut through the thigh joint between turkey drumstick and thigh to separate. Season.
3 Heat oil in a large frying pan over medium heat; cook drumstick and thigh, one piece at a time, until browned. Transfer to the slow cooker; placing the thigh on the base and the drumstick on top.
4 Melt 20g of the butter in the same frying pan over medium heat. Add chopped onion, garlic, bacon and celery; cook, stirring, until bacon is browned. Transfer to a large bowl; cool slightly. Add breadcrumbs, egg and sage; stir to combine.
5 Grease two 30cm x 40cm (12 inch x 16 inch) pieces of foil. Divide bacon mixture evenly between foil sheets; shape each into a 20cm (8 inch) log. Roll up to enclose. Place foil parcels around turkey.
6 Cook, covered, on low, for 8 hours. Remove foil parcels and turkey from the cooker. Cover to keep warm.
7 Strain cooking liquid into a medium heatproof jug; reserve onion. Skim fat from surface. Add enough of the water to make 2½ cups of liquid.
8 Melt remaining butter in a medium saucepan over medium heat; cook the reserved onion, stirring, until browned. Add flour; cook, stirring, until mixture thickens and bubbles. Gradually add cooking liquid; stir until mixture boils and thickens.
9 Slice turkey; serve with gravy, seasoning and cranberry sauce.

serving suggestion Serve with roasted potatoes and pumpkin, or mash, and steamed broccoli or green beans.
tips Turkey is often sold frozen in larger supermarkets. Allow at least one day to thaw in the refrigerator before using. If you can't find a turkey hindquarter use two turkey drumsticks (often called turkey shanks), or use turkey breast on the bone, (called turkey buffe).
You can serve the turkey with the strained and seasoned juices instead of making the gravy.

Not suitable to freeze.

nutritional count per serving
- 42.3g total fat
- 16.6g saturated fat
- 3205kJ (766 cal)
- 31.6g carbohydrate
- 64.6g protein
- 2.4g fibre

BEEF & VEAL

pho bo

PREP + COOK TIME 6 HOURS **SERVES** 4

1kg (2 pounds) chopped beef bones

1 large brown onion (200g), chopped coarsely

5cm (2-inch) piece fresh ginger (25g), chopped coarsely

2.5 litres (10-cups) boiling water

6 star anise

2 cinnamon sticks

10 cloves

2 tablespoons coriander seeds

¼ cup (60ml) fish sauce

¼ cup (60ml) lime juice

2 tablespoons brown sugar

200g (6½ ounces) rice stick noodles

250g (8 ounces) beef eye fillet, sliced thinly

2 cups (160g) bean sprouts

½ cup firmly packed fresh mint

½ cup firmly packed fresh coriander (cilantro)

½ cup firmly packed fresh vietnamese mint leaves

2 fresh long red chillies, sliced thinly

1 Place bones, onion and ginger in a 4.5-litre (18-cup) slow cooker. Cook, covered, on high, for 2 hours.

2 Add the water, star anise, cinnamon, cloves and coriander seeds. Cook, covered, on high, for 3 hours. Add sauce, juice and sugar. Strain cooking liquid through a muslin-lined sieve, clean chux or linen tea towel; discard solids.

3 Place noodles in a medium heatproof bowl, cover with boiling water; stand for 15 minutes or until softened; drain.

4 Divide noodles and beef among serving bowls. Ladle hot soup over noodles; scatter over sprouts, mint, fresh coriander, vietnamese mint and chilli to serve.

Suitable to freeze at the end of step 2.

nutritional count per serving
- 3.7g total fat
- 1.3g saturated fat
- 695kJ (166 cal)
- 14.6g carbohydrate
- 17.1g protein
- 3.1g fibre

BEEF & VEAL

steak and pepper dumpling pie

PREP + COOK TIME 8¾ HOURS SERVES 6

1.2kg (2½-pounds) beef chuck steak
12 shallots (300g), unpeeled
2½ tablespoons olive oil
2 cloves garlic, crushed
4 rindless bacon rashers (250g), chopped coarsely
400g (12½ ounces) button mushrooms, halved
2 teaspoons cracked black pepper
1 tablespoon plain (all-purpose) flour
2 tablespoons tomato paste
1½ cups (225g) self-raising flour
75g (2½ ounces) cold butter, chopped finely
¼ cup finely chopped fresh flat-leaf parsley
½ cup (40g) finely grated parmesan cheese
¾ cup (180ml) milk, approximately

1 Cut beef into 3cm (1¼-inch) pieces. Peel shallots leaving root end intact.

2 Heat 1½ tablespoons oil in a large frying pan over medium-high heat. Cook beef, in three batches, until browned. Transfer to a 4.5-litre (18-cup) slow cooker.

3 Heat remaining oil in the same pan; cook shallots, garlic, bacon and mushrooms, stirring, for 10 minutes or until shallots soften. Add pepper and plain flour; cook, stirring, for 1 minute. Add paste; stir to combine. Transfer mixture to slow cooker. Cook, covered, on low, for 7 hours. Season with salt.

BEEF & VEAL

4 Place self-raising flour in a medium bowl; rub in butter. Add parsley and cheese; stir to combine. Stir in enough milk to make a soft, sticky dough. Roll dough into a 30cm (12-inch) square on a lightly floured surface. Roll up to form a log shape; trim ends. Slice into 2cm (¾-inch) thick rounds. Place rounds, in a single layer, over beef mixture. Cook, covered, a further 1 hour or until dumplings are risen and cooked through.

serving suggestion Steamed green beans.

Suitable to freeze at the end of step 3.

nutritional count per serving
▸ 43.8g total fat
▸ 17.2g saturated fat
▸ 3223kJ (770 cal)
▸ 29.4g carbohydrate
▸ 64.3g protein
▸ 6.5g fibre

moroccan beef meatballs

PREP + COOK TIME 6¾ HOURS SERVES 6

2 slices white bread (90g)
½ cup (125ml) milk
1kg (2 pounds) minced (ground) beef
1 egg
2 tablespoons finely chopped fresh coriander (cilantro) roots and stems
1 tablespoon ground cumin
1 tablespoon ground coriander
1 tablespoon sweet paprika
2 teaspoons ground ginger
1 teaspoon ground cinnamon
1 large brown onion (200g), chopped finely
4 cloves garlic, chopped finely
1 tablespoon olive oil
2 tablespoons tomato paste
700g (1½-pounds) bottled passata
½ cup (125ml) beef stock
2 tablespoons honey
½ cup firmly packed fresh coriander leaves (cilantro)

1 Remove and discard crusts from bread. Combine bread and milk in a small bowl; stand for 10 minutes.
2 Combine bread mixture, beef, egg, coriander root and stem mixture, cumin, ground coriander, paprika, ginger, cinnamon, and half of the onion and garlic, in a large bowl; roll level tablespoons of mixture into balls, place in a 4.5-litre (18-cup) slow cooker.
3 Heat oil in a large frying pan over medium heat. Cook the remaining onion and garlic, stirring, for 5 minutes or until onion softens. Stir in paste, passata, stock and honey; transfer to slow cooker. Cook, covered, on low, for 6 hours. Season to taste. Sprinkle with fresh coriander to serve.

serving suggestion Couscous and greek-style yoghurt.
tip Passata is sieved tomato puree available from most supermarkets.

Suitable to freeze at the end of step 3 without coriander.

---

nutritional count per serving
▶ 18.6g total fat
▶ 7.5g saturated fat
▶ 1570kJ (375 cal)
▶ 12.7g carbohydrate
▶ 38.4g protein
▶ 2g fibre

In Italian, osso buco literally means 'bone with a hole'. It is cut from the shin of the hind leg (shank), and is also known as knuckle. The hole is filled with rich bone marrow, also known as 'jelly'; stand the bones upright to cook, so you don't lose the delicious jelly inside.

tuscan beef stew

PREP + COOK TIME 6½ HOURS SERVES 6

6 pieces beef osso buco (1.2kg)
1 tablespoon olive oil
1 large brown onion (200g), chopped coarsely
3 cloves garlic, crushed
6 anchovy fillets, drained, chopped finely
2 tablespoons plain (all-purpose) flour
¼ cup (60ml) balsamic vinegar
2 tablespoons tomato paste
400g (12½ ounces) canned crushed tomatoes
1 cup (250ml) beef stock
¼ cup (60ml) water
4 sprigs fresh rosemary
1 cup (120g) pitted green olives

1 Trim excess fat from the beef. Heat oil in a large frying pan over medium-high heat. Cook beef, in batches, until browned. Transfer to a 4.5-litre (18-cup) slow cooker.
2 Add onion, garlic and anchovy to same pan; cook, stirring, 1 minute or until fragrant. Add flour; cook, stirring, 1 minute. Stir in vinegar and paste, then tomatoes, stock, the water and rosemary. Transfer mixture to slow cooker.
3 Cook, covered, on low, 6 hours. Season to taste. Just before serving, stir in olives.

serving suggestion Soft polenta and baby rocket leaves.

Suitable to freeze at the end of step 3.

nutritional count per serving
▶ 8.2g total fat
▶ 1.9g saturated fat
▶ 1437kJ (343 cal)
▶ 9g carbohydrate
▶ 55.7g protein
▶ 2.5g fibre

BEEF & VEAL

veal with marsala and mushrooms

PREP + COOK TIME 6½ HOURS SERVES 6

300g (9½ ounces) button mushrooms

¼ cup (35g) plain (all-purpose) flour

6 pieces veal osso buco (1.5kg)

1 tablespoon olive oil

20g (¾ ounce) butter

6 shallots (150g), chopped finely

2 cloves garlic, chopped finely

½ cup (125ml) marsala

2 cups (500ml) salt-reduced beef stock

½ cup (125ml) pouring cream

1 tablespoon wholegrain mustard

¼ cup coarsely chopped fresh flat-leaf parsley

1 Place mushrooms over base of a 4.5-litre (18-cup) slow cooker.
2 Reserve 1 tablespoon flour. Toss veal in remaining flour to coat, shake off excess. Heat oil and butter in a large frying pan over medium-high heat. Cook veal, in batches, until browned. Transfer to slow cooker.
3 Cook shallot and garlic in the same pan, stirring, for about 5 minutes or until shallot is softened. Add reserved flour; cook, stirring, for 1 minute. Stir in marsala and stock; bring to the boil. Transfer to slow cooker.
4 Cook, covered, on low, for 6 hours. Carefully remove veal from cooker; cover to keep warm.
5 Add cream and mustard to cooker; stir to combine. Cook, covered, on high, for 10 minutes or until heated through. Season to taste. Sprinkle with parsley to serve.

Suitable to freeze at the end of step 4.

nutritional count per serving
- 14.2g total fat
- 7.2g saturated fat
- 874kJ (201 cal)
- 10.2g carbohydrate
- 4.8g protein
- 2.2g fibre

serving suggestion
Serve with mashed potato, soft polenta, buttered pasta or risotto, and steamed green vegetables.

nutritional count per serving
- 25.1g total fat
- 12g saturated fat
- 2071kJ (495 cal)
- 24.7g carbohydrate
- 38g protein
- 4.4g fibre

beef casserole with cheesy herb dumplings

PREP + COOK TIME 8½ HOURS **SERVES** 6

1kg (2 pounds) gravy beef
1 tablespoon olive oil
1 large brown onion (200g), chopped coarsely
2 cloves garlic, crushed
2 tablespoons tomato paste
400g (12½ ounces) canned whole peeled tomatoes
1 cup (250ml) beef stock
½ cup (125ml) dry red wine
4 sprigs fresh thyme
250g (8 ounces) button mushrooms, halved
1 cup (150g) self-raising flour
50g (1½ ounces) cold butter, chopped finely
2 tablespoons finely chopped fresh flat-leaf parsley
⅔ cup (80g) coarsely grated vintage cheddar cheese
½ cup (125ml) buttermilk, approximately

1 Cut beef into 3cm (1¼-inch) pieces. Heat oil in a large frying pan over medium-high heat. Cook beef, in batches, until browned. Transfer to a 4.5-litre (18-cup) slow cooker.
2 Add onion and garlic to same pan; cook, stirring, 5 minutes or until onion softens. Add paste, tomatoes, stock, wine and thyme to pan; bring to the boil. Transfer mixture to slow cooker; add mushrooms.
3 Cook, covered, on low, for 7 hours. Remove and discard thyme sprigs. Season to taste.
4 Meanwhile, place flour in a medium bowl; rub in butter. Add half of the parsley and half of the cheese; stir to combine. Stir in enough buttermilk to make a soft, sticky dough. Drop rounded tablespoons of the dumpling mixture, 2cm (¾-inch) apart, on top of the casserole; scatter with remaining cheese. Cook, covered, 1 hour or until dumplings are cooked through. Scatter with remaining parsley to serve.

tip We used a cabernet-style wine in this recipe.

Suitable to freeze at the end of step 3.

BEEF & VEAL

Short ribs, although they're not necessarily that short, are sections of beef ribs, not pork, usually taken from the second to the 10th rib. Each 'slab' can contain from two to eight ribs. The meat is full of flavour, but is very tough, so the ribs are best braised slowly over low heat, making them perfect for cooking in a slow cooker.

bourbon-glazed beef ribs

PREP + COOK TIME 8½ HOURS SERVES 4

1 medium brown onion (150g), chopped finely
5 cloves garlic, chopped coarsely
½ cup (140g) tomato sauce (ketchup)
½ cup (140g) sweet chilli sauce
⅓ cup (80ml) light soy sauce
½ cup (125ml) bourbon
½ cup (175g) honey
8 beef short ribs (2kg)

1 Combine onion, garlic, sauces, bourbon and honey in a 4.5-litre (18-cup) slow cooker. Add beef; turn to coat in mixture. Cook, covered, on low, for 8 hours.
2 Carefully remove beef from cooker; cover to keep warm. Transfer sauce to a large frying pan; bring to the boil. Boil, skimming fat from surface, for about 10 minutes or until sauce reduces to 2 cups.
3 Spoon sauce over beef to serve.

serving suggestion Thinly sliced fried potatoes.

Suitable to freeze at the end of step 3.

nutritional count per serving
- 20.7g total fat
- 7.8g saturated fat
- 3087kJ (738 cal)
- 47g carbohydrate
- 75.5g protein
- 0.1g fibre

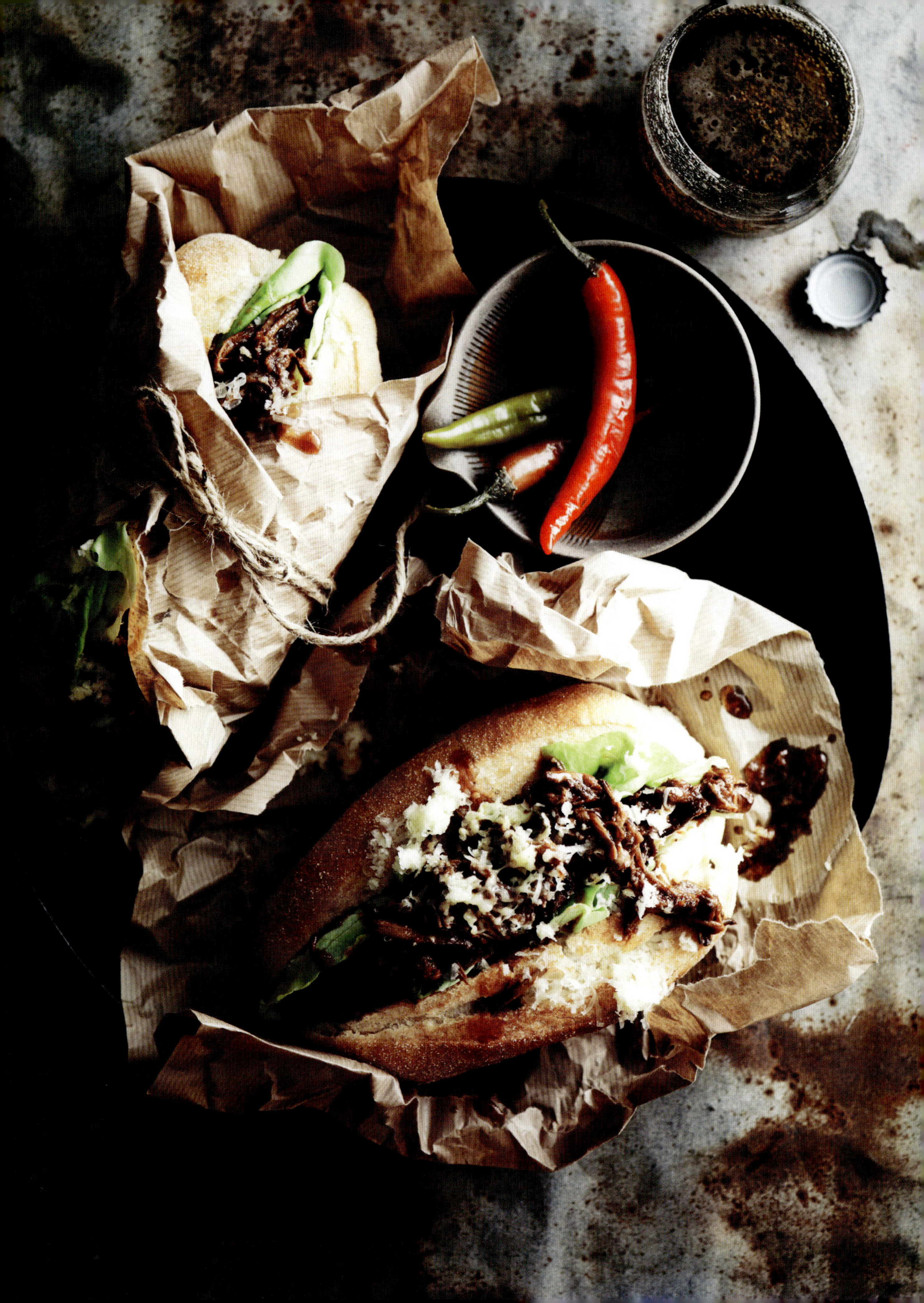

BEEF & VEAL

Pulled beef, or pork, comes from pulling extremely tender pieces of meat apart – rather than cutting it into slices – usually with two forks, which separates the meat into strands. Low, slow cooking is required to get meat tender enough to be able to pull it apart into pieces.

pulled beef with barbecue sauce

PREP + COOK TIME 8¾ HOURS SERVES 6

2 cloves garlic, crushed
1 fresh long red chilli, chopped finely
2 tablespoons dark brown sugar
1½ cups (420g) tomato sauce (ketchup)
1½ tablespoons worcestershire sauce
2 tablespoons cider vinegar
750g (1½-pound) piece beef rump
6 long crusty bread rolls

1 Place garlic, chilli, sugar, sauces and vinegar in a 4.5-litre (18-cup) slow cooker. Stir well to combine; add beef and turn to coat in mixture. Cook, covered, on low, for 8 hours.
2 Carefully remove beef from cooker; shred meat coarsely using two forks.
3 Transfer sauce mixture to a large saucepan, bring to the boil over medium heat. Boil, uncovered, for about 10 minutes or until thickened. Stir in beef.
4 Split rolls in half horizontally. Sandwich beef and sauce mixture between rolls.

serving suggestion Fill rolls with beef mixture, lettuce, cheddar and pickled peppers.

Suitable to freeze at the end of step 2.

nutritional count per serving
▶ 8.9g total fat
▶ 2.6g saturated fat
▶ 2159kJ (516 cal)
▶ 70.4g carbohydrate
▶ 36g protein
▶ 5.8g fibre

BEEF & VEAL

chinese braised beef cheeks

PREP + COOK TIME 8½ HOURS SERVES 8

4 green onions (scallions)

1 large orange

6 cloves garlic, crushed

10cm (4-inch) piece fresh ginger (50g), sliced thickly

1½ cups (375ml) chinese cooking wine

1 cup (250ml) soy sauce

1 cup (220g) brown sugar

½ teaspoon sesame oil

5 star anise

2 cinnamon sticks

8 beef cheeks (2.5kg)

1 fresh long red chilli, sliced thinly

2 green onions (scallions), extra, trimmed, sliced thinly lengthways

½ cup firmly packed fresh coriander leaves (cilantro)

1 Trim onions; cut into 6cm (2½-inch) lengths. Using a vegetable peeler, peel 3 wide strips of rind from orange (save fruit to eat later, if you like).
2 Combine onion, rind, garlic, ginger, wine, sauce, sugar, oil, star anise and cinnamon in a 4.5-litre (18-cup) slow cooker. Stir until the sugar dissolves. Add beef; turn to coat in mixture. Cook, covered, on low, for 8 hours.
3 Serve beef with a little cooking liquid; sprinkle with chilli, extra onion and coriander.

serving suggestion Serve with steamed rice.

Suitable to freeze at the end of step 2.

nutritional count per serving
▶ 12.7g total fat
▶ 5.4g saturated fat
▶ 1521kJ (366 cal)
▶ 29g carbohydrate
▶ 34.7g protein
▶ 0.8g fibre

test kitchen tip
You may need to order beef cheeks in advance from the butcher.

test kitchen tip
You will need about 2 large bunches of coriander.

coriander beef curry

PREP + COOK TIME 8½ HOURS SERVES 6

1.5kg (3 pounds) chuck steak or gravy beef
6 fresh long green chillies
7.5cm (3-inch) piece fresh ginger (35g), chopped coarsely
4 cloves garlic, chopped coarsely
2 medium tomatoes (300g), chopped coarsely
1 tablespoon tomato paste
2 teaspoons sea salt flakes
2½ cups firmly packed fresh coriander leaves (cilantro)
1½ tablespoons vegetable oil
400ml (14 ounces) canned coconut cream

1 Cut beef into 5cm (2-inch) pieces.
2 Coarsely chop four chillies. Thinly slice remaining chillies, reserve.
3 Blend or process chopped chilli, ginger, garlic, fresh tomato, tomato paste, salt and 2 cups of the coriander until smooth. Reserve ½ cup of the paste; cover, then refrigerate.
4 Heat 1 tablespoon of the oil in a large frying pan over medium-high heat; cook beef, in batches, until browned. Transfer beef to a 4.5-litre (18-cup) slow cooker.
5 Add the remaining coriander paste mixture and 1 cup of the coconut cream to the slow cooker; stir to combine. (Refrigerate remaining coconut cream.) Cook, covered, on low, for 8 hours. Season to taste.
6 Heat remaining oil in a small frying pan; cook sliced chillies, stirring, for 2 minutes or until softened. Drizzle curry with the remaining coconut cream; top with reserved coriander paste, chilli and remaining coriander.

serving suggestion Steamed jasmine rice.

Suitable to freeze at the end of step 5.

nutritional count per serving
▶ 36.4g total fat
▶ 18.4g saturated fat
▶ 2424kJ (579 cal)
▶ 4.9g carbohydrate
▶ 57.6g protein
▶ 2.3g fibre

LAMB

lamb shank and spinach korma curry

PREP + COOK TIME 8½ **HOURS** **SERVES** 6

6 french-trimmed lamb shanks (1.5kg)
400g (12½ ounces) canned crushed tomatoes
1 large brown onion (200g), sliced thickly
300ml (½ pint) pouring cream
100g (3 ounces) baby spinach leaves
1 cup (120g) frozen peas

KORMA PASTE
1 tablespoon cumin seeds
3 cloves garlic, quartered
5cm (2-inch) piece fresh ginger (25g), grated finely
⅓ cup (50g) toasted cashew nuts
¼ cup (60ml) tomato sauce (ketchup)
¼ cup coarsely chopped coriander (cilantro) root and stem
2 tablespoons desiccated coconut
1 tablespoon garam masala
2 teaspoons ground coriander
2 teaspoons ground turmeric
2 teaspoons sea salt flakes
¼ cup (60ml) vegetable oil

1 Make korma paste.
2 Combine lamb, tomatoes, onion, cream and paste in a 4.5-litre (18-cup) slow cooker. Cook, covered, on low, for 8 hours.
3 Add spinach and peas to cooker; cook, covered, for 10 minutes or until heated through.

KORMA PASTE Place cumin in a small frying pan; cook, stirring, for 1 minute or until fragrant. Remove from heat. Blend or process cumin with remaining ingredients until smooth.

Korma paste is suitable to freeze.

nutritional count per serving
- 44.3g total fat
- 19.3g saturated fat
- 2473kJ (34 cal)
- 12.9g carbohydrate
- 34g protein
- 4.6g fibre

serving suggestion
Steamed basmati rice, yoghurt, and a flatbread such as naan.

fetta, lemon and herb rolled lamb

PREP + COOK TIME 8¾ HOURS SERVES 6

180g (5½ ounces) persian fetta in oil

¼ cup coarsely chopped fresh oregano

¼ cup coarsely chopped fresh mint

¼ cup coarsely chopped fresh basil

2 teaspoons finely grated lemon rind

2 tablespoons balsamic vinegar

1.5kg (3-pound) boned leg of lamb

1 Drain fetta reserving 2 tablespoons of the oil.
2 Combine fetta, herbs, rind and half the vinegar in a medium bowl. Season to taste.
3 Open out lamb and place on a board, fat-side down. Slice through the thickest part of the lamb horizontally, without cutting all the way through. Open out the flap to form one large even piece; spread fetta mixture over lamb. Roll lamb up to enclose the stuffing, securing with kitchen string at 2cm (¾-inch) intervals.
4 Heat half the reserved oil in a large frying pan over medium-high heat; cook lamb, turning, until browned. Transfer to a 4.5-litre (18-cup) slow cooker.

LAMB

Persian fetta is a soft, creamy cheese marinated in a blend of olive oil, garlic, herbs and spices. It is available from most major supermarkets. Ask the butcher to butterfly the lamb for you.

5 Combine remaining reserved oil and vinegar in a small bowl; brush all over lamb. Cook, covered, on low, for 8 hours.

serving suggestion Roasted wedges of pumpkin and fresh garden peas; sprinkle with extra fresh herbs, if you like.

Not suitable to freeze.

> **nutritional count per serving**
> ▶ 24.3g total fat
> ▶ 11.1g saturated fat
> ▶ 1957kJ (467 cal)
> ▶ 35g carbohydrate
> ▶ 58.2g protein
> ▶ 0.3g fibre

LAMB

lamb, spinach and chickpea rice pilaf

PREP + COOK TIME 8½ HOURS SERVES 6

1kg (2-pound) boned lamb shoulder

2 tablespoons olive oil

1 large brown onion (200g), sliced thinly

4 cloves garlic, crushed

1 tablespoon ground cumin

1 tablespoon ground coriander

2 teaspoons ground allspice

2 teaspoons chilli powder

3 cups (750ml) chicken stock

2 cups (400g) basmati rice

1 bunch silver beet (1kg), trimmed, chopped coarsely

400g (12½ ounces) canned chickpeas (garbanzo beans), rinsed, drained

⅔ cup (100g) raisins

½ cup (80g) pine nuts, toasted

½ cup coarsely chopped fresh coriander (cilantro)

1 Cut lamb into 2cm (¾-inch) pieces. Heat half the oil in a large frying pan over medium heat; cook lamb, in batches, until browned. Transfer to a 4.5-litre (18-cup) slow cooker.

2 Heat remaining oil in the same pan; cook onion and garlic, stirring, for 5 minutes or until onion softens. Add spices; cook, stirring, for 1 minute or until fragrant. Stir in stock; bring to the boil. Transfer mixture to the slow cooker. Cook, covered, on low, for 7 hours.

3 Stir in rice; top with silver beet and chickpeas. Cook, covered, on high, for 50 minutes. Season to taste.

4 Stir in raisins, pine nuts and coriander to serve.

serving suggestion Accompany with greek-style yoghurt and lemon wedges.

Suitable to freeze at the end of step 2.

nutritional count per serving
- 27.7g total fat
- 6.5g saturated fat
- 2507kJ (599 cal)
- 41.7g carbohydrate
- 43.9g protein
- 5.9g fibre

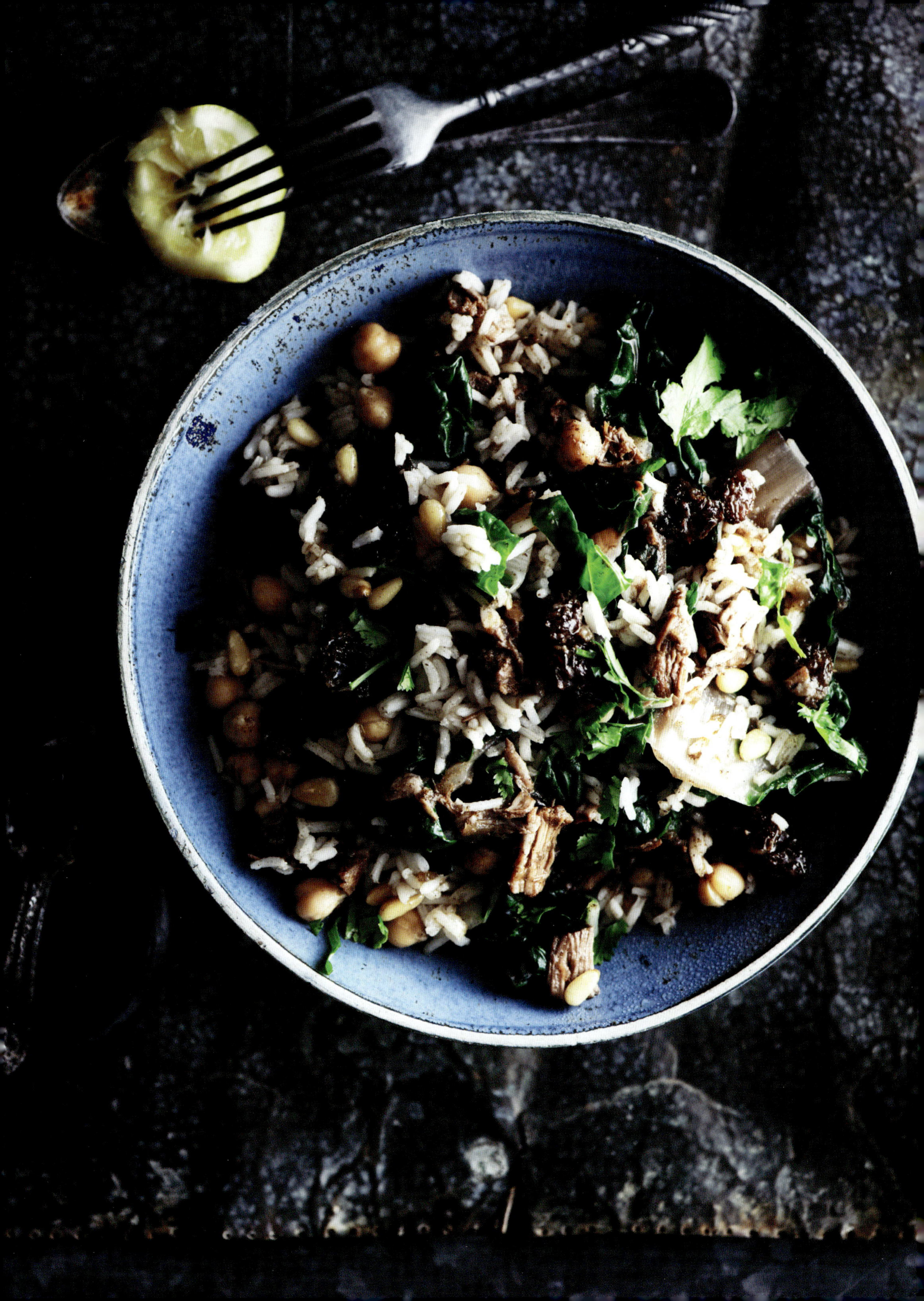

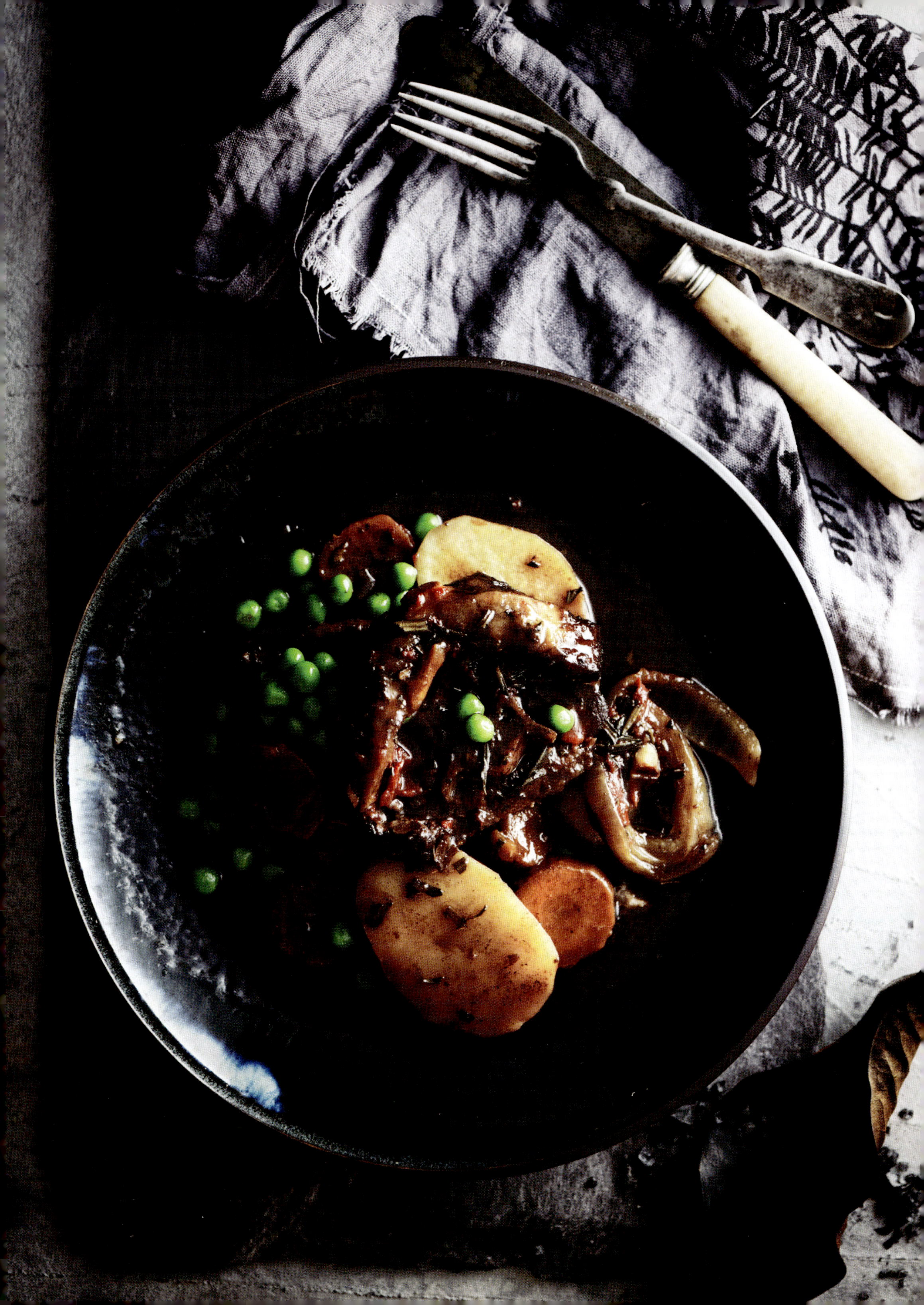

lamb and rosemary stew

PREP + COOK TIME 8¾ HOURS SERVES 4

1.2kg (2½ pounds) lamb neck chops
⅓ cup (50g) plain (all-purpose) flour
2 tablespoons olive oil
1 cup (250ml) dry red wine
3 small brown onions (240g), sliced thickly
3 medium potatoes (600g), sliced thickly
2 medium carrots (240g), sliced thickly
2 tablespoons tomato paste
2 tablespoons finely chopped rosemary
1 cup (250ml) beef stock

1 Toss lamb in flour to coat; shake off excess. Heat half the oil in a large frying pan over medium-high heat; cook lamb, in batches, until browned. Transfer to a 4.5-litre (18-cup) slow cooker.

2 Add wine to the same pan; bring to the boil. Boil, stirring occasionally, for about 5 minutes or until liquid is reduced by half. Transfer to slow cooker. Add onion, potato, carrot, paste, rosemary and stock. Cook, covered, on low, for 8 hours.

3 Divide lamb and vegetables among plates. Spoon over a little cooking liquid to serve.

serving suggestion Peas or green beans.
tip We used a shiraz-style wine in this recipe.

Suitable to freeze at the end of step 2.

nutritional count per serving
▶ 44.5g total fat
▶ 17.5g saturated fat
▶ 3072kJ (734 cal)
▶ 32.3g carbohydrate
▶ 41.8g protein
▶ 5.9g fibre

LAMB

greek-style dill and lemon lamb shoulder

PREP + COOK TIME 8¾ HOURS SERVES 6

1 tablespoon olive oil

2kg (4-pound) lamb shoulder, bone in

1 medium lemon (140g)

4 cloves garlic, crushed

2 teaspoons dried greek oregano

1 tablespoon coarsely chopped fresh dill

800g (1½ pounds) potatoes, cut into thick wedges

1 cup (280g) bottled passata

2 cups (500ml) salt-reduced chicken stock

50g (1½ ounces) pitted black olives

2 tablespoons fresh dill sprigs, extra

1 Heat oil in a large frying pan over medium heat; cook lamb until browned all over. Remove from pan.
2 Meanwhile, finely grate rind from lemon; reserve lemon. Combine garlic, rind, oregano and chopped dill in a small bowl. Rub mixture all over lamb.
3 Place potato over the base of a 4.5-litre (18-cup) slow cooker. Pour passata and stock over the potatoes. Top with lamb. Cook, covered, on low, for 8 hours.
4 Carefully remove lamb and potato from the cooker; shred the lamb coarsely using two forks. Cover to keep warm.
5 Pour cooking liquid into a medium saucepan; bring to the boil. Boil, uncovered, about 10 minutes or until liquid is reduced by half. Add olives; cook until heated through. Season to taste.
6 Cut reserved lemon into wedges. Serve lamb with potato, pan juices and lemon wedges; sprinkle with extra dill. Drizzle lamb with a little greek-style yoghurt before serving, if you like.

serving suggestion Steamed broad beans.

Suitable to freeze at the end of step 2.

test kitchen tips

Ask the butcher to separate the shank from the shoulder, leaving it attached; this will help it fit into the cooker. We used dutch cream potatoes in this recipe, as they hold their shape well. Passata is sieved tomato puree available from supermarkets.

nutritional count per serving
- 20g total fat
- 7.5g saturated fat
- 2035kJ (486 cal)
- 20.3g carbohydrate
- 53.8g protein
- 3g fibre

test kitchen tip
Ask the butcher to butterfly the lamb for you.

lamb with sage and prosciutto

PREP + COOK TIME 8¾ HOURS SERVES 6

1 large brown onion (200g), chopped coarsely
2 stalks celery (300g), trimmed, chopped coarsely
1 large carrot (180g), chopped coarsely
½ cup (125ml) dry red wine
1.5kg (3-pound) boned lamb shoulder
¼ cup loosely packed fresh sage leaves
4 cloves garlic, sliced thinly
12 thin slices prosciutto (180g)

1 Transfer onion, celery, carrot and wine to a 4.5-litre (18-cup) slow cooker.
2 Open out the lamb and place on a board, fat-side down. Slice through the thickest part of the lamb horizontally, without cutting all the way through. Open out the flap to form one large even piece; season, then scatter over sage and garlic. Roll lamb up to enclose seasoning. Wrap prosciutto around lamb, securing with kitchen string at 2cm (¾-inch) intervals. Transfer lamb to slow cooker. Cook, covered, on low, for 8 hours.
3 Carefully remove lamb from cooker; cover to keep warm. Strain sauce into a medium saucepan. Discard solids. Bring to the boil over medium heat; boil, uncovered, for 5 minutes or until sauce has reduced to ¾ cup. Drizzle lamb with sauce.

serving suggestion Roasted root vegetables.
tip We used a shiraz-style wine in this recipe.

Not suitable to freeze.

nutritional count per serving
▶ 19.6g total fat
▶ 8.3g saturated fat
▶ 1875kJ (448 cal)
▶ 5.4g carbohydrate
▶ 58.7g protein
▶ 2.3g fibre

cassoulet

PREP + COOK TIME 8¾ HOURS SERVES 6

100g (3-ounce) piece speck

2 tablespoons olive oil

3 thick pork sausages (360g)

900g (1¾ pounds) boned lamb shoulder

1 large brown onion (200g), chopped finely

1 bay leaf

5 cloves garlic, chopped finely

2 x 400g (12½-ounce) cans diced tomatoes

1 cup (250ml) water

2 tablespoons tomato paste

4 x 400g (12½-ounce) cans white beans, rinsed, drained

2 tablespoons finely chopped fresh flat-leaf parsley

1 Discard the rind from the speck. Cut the speck into 3cm (1¼-inch) squares.

2 Heat half the oil in a large frying pan over medium-high heat; cook sausages and speck, turning, until browned. Transfer to a 4.5-litre (18-cup) slow cooker.

3 Cut the lamb into 3cm (1¼-inch) pieces. Heat the same pan over medium-high heat; cook lamb, in batches, until browned. Transfer to slow cooker. Drain fat from pan.

4 Heat remaining oil in the same pan over medium heat; cook onion and bay leaf, stirring, for 5 minutes or until onion softens. Add garlic; cook, stirring, for 1 minute or until fragrant. Transfer to slow cooker.

5 Add tomatoes, the water, paste and beans to cooker. Cook, covered, on low, for 8 hours. Serve sprinkled with parsley.

tip For a twist, lightly toast some breadcrumbs and combine with the chopped parsley; sprinkle over cassoulet to serve.

Suitable to freeze at the end of step 5.

nutritional count per serving
- 35.7g total fat
- 13.4g saturated fat
- 2575kJ (615 cal)
- 19.3g carbohydrate
- 50.8g protein
- 9.8g fibre

test kitchen tip

There are many regional variations of cassoulet in France. For special occasions, you could add two confit duck marylands. Pan fry them until hot and browned, and place on top of the hot cassoulet before sprinkling over the parsley.

test kitchen tip

Place the meat, salad, bread, yoghurt and harissa on the table and let everyone make their own wrap. You could also serve the lamb wrap with sliced cucumber, fresh mint or parsley leaves, and hummus.

nutritional count per serving
- 18.4g total fat
- 8.4g saturated fat
- 2425kJ (579 cal)
- 40.3g carbohydrate
- 59g protein
- 4.3g fibre

turkish lamb shawarma

Shawarma usually refers to meat cooked on a turning spit, but it also refers to a pitta bread sandwich. This is our slow cooker take on the shawarma.

PREP + COOK TIME 8½ HOURS SERVES 8

8 cloves garlic, crushed

3 teaspoons each ground cumin, cinnamon, coriander and paprika

1½ teaspoons each ground cardamom, nutmeg and allspice

1 teaspoon ground white pepper

2kg (4-pound) boned lamb shoulder

1 cup (250ml) chicken stock

2 baby cos (romaine) lettuce (360g)

1 large red onion (300g)

4 medium tomatoes (600g)

16 pocket pitta breads

1 Combine garlic and spices in a small bowl. Rub spice mixture over the lamb. Transfer lamb to a 4.5-litre (18-cup) slow cooker; pour over the stock. Cook, covered, on low, 8 hours.
2 Just before ready to serve, trim and finely shred the lettuce. Peel and thinly slice the onion; thinly slice the tomato. Place lettuce, onion and tomato in separate serving bowls. Warm bread under a preheated grill or in a microwave.
3 Using two forks, shred lamb coarsely; place in a serving bowl. Spoon over a little of the cooking liquid. Serve lamb with lettuce, onion, tomato and pitta.

serving suggestion Accompany with greek-style yoghurt and, if you can tolerate it, harissa, a fiery Moroccan paste.

Suitable to freeze at the end of step 1.

LAMB

lancashire hot pot

PREP + COOK TIME 8½ HOURS SERVES 4

800g (1½-pound) boned lamb shoulder
⅓ cup (50g) plain (all-purpose) flour
2 tablespoons olive oil
2 medium brown onions (300g), chopped coarsely
2 cloves garlic, chopped coarsely
½ cup (125ml) dry red wine
2 medium carrots (240g), chopped coarsely
200g (6½ ounces) button mushrooms, halved
1 tablespoon fresh thyme leaves
1 tablespoon worcestershire sauce
500g (1 pound) potatoes

1 Cut lamb into 3cm (1¼-inch) pieces. Toss in flour to coat, shake off excess. Heat half the oil in a large frying pan over medium-high heat; cook lamb, in batches, until browned. Transfer to a 4.5-litre (18-cup) slow cooker.

2 Heat remaining oil in the same pan; cook onion and garlic, stirring, for 5 minutes or until onion softens. Transfer to slow cooker.

3 Heat same pan; add wine, bring to the boil. Transfer to cooker with carrot, mushrooms, thyme and sauce; stir to combine.

4 Thinly slice potatoes. Arrange potato slices, slightly overlapping, over lamb mixture. Cook, covered, on low, for 8 hours. Season to taste.

serving suggestion Buttered peas.

Not suitable to freeze.

nutritional count per serving
▶ 21.1g total fat
▶ 6.9g saturated fat
▶ 2225kJ (532 cal)
▶ 30.4g carbohydrate
▶ 47.5g protein
▶ 6.8g fibre

test kitchen tips
If you have one, try using a mandoline to cut the potatoes into paper-thin slices, otherwise, use a very sharp knife.
We used a merlot-style wine in this recipe.

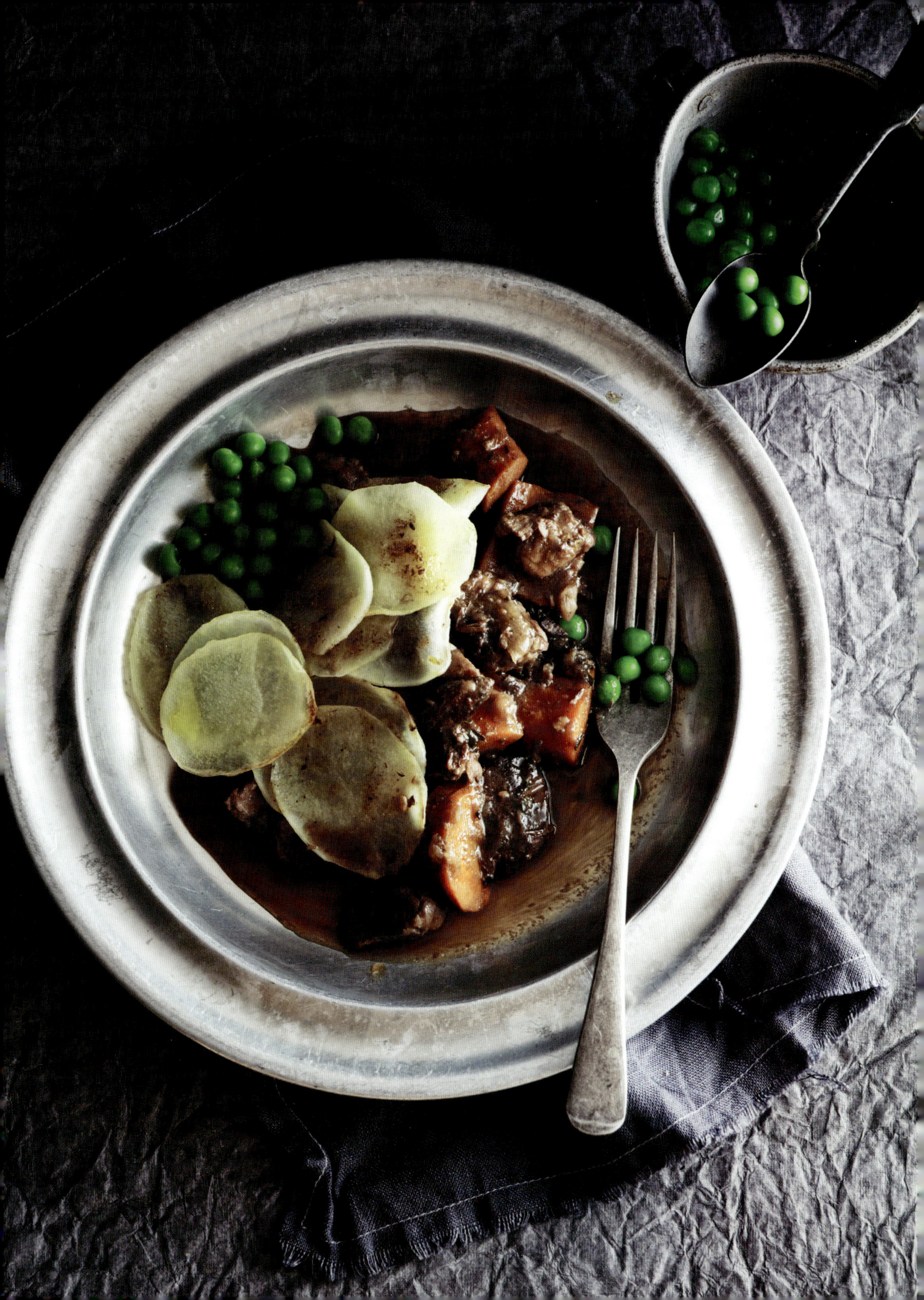

test kitchen tip

Sprinkle the curry with fried chillies before serving, if you like. To fry the chillies, thinly slice 2 fresh long red chillies. Heat 2 teaspoons oil in a small frying pan, and cook the chillies, stirring, until softened.

lamb and baby eggplant curry with cashew and coconut

PREP + COOK TIME 8¾ HOURS SERVES 6

6 baby eggplants (360g)

¼ cup (60ml) vegetable oil

6 french-trimmed lamb shanks (1.5kg)

1 large brown onion (200g), chopped finely

3 cloves garlic, grated

5cm (2-inch) piece fresh ginger (25g)

3 fresh long red chillies, sliced thinly

2 teaspoons each ground cumin, coriander and garam masala

400g (12½ ounces) canned diced tomatoes

2 cups (500ml) beef stock

1 tablespoon sesame seeds

¼ cup (50g) toasted salted cashews

1 tablespoon desiccated coconut

¾ cup (200g) greek-style yoghurt

¼ cup lightly packed fresh coriander leaves (cilantro)

1 Cut the eggplants into 3cm (1¼-inch) thick slices. Heat 1 tablespoon of the oil in a large frying pan over medium heat; cook eggplant, in batches, until browned. Transfer to a 4.5-litre (18-cup) slow cooker.

2 Heat 1 tablespoon of the oil in the same pan over medium heat; cook the lamb, in batches, until browned. Transfer to the slow cooker.

3 Heat remaining oil in the same pan over medium heat; cook onion, stirring, for 5 minutes or until softened. Add garlic, ginger, chilli and spices; cook, stirring, for 1 minute or until fragrant. Stir in tomatoes and stock; bring to the boil. Transfer to the slow cooker. Cook, covered, on low, for 8 hours.

4 Meanwhile, dry-fry seeds, nuts and coconut together until fragrant but not coloured; cool. Blend or process until finely ground. Stir nut mixture into curry. Season to taste.

5 Serve curry topped with yoghurt and coriander.

serving suggestion Steamed basmati rice and asian greens.

Suitable to freeze at the end of step 3.

---

nutritional count per serving
- 31g total fat
- 10g saturated fat
- 1968kJ (470 cal)
- 12.1g carbohydrate
- 34.1g protein
- 4.2g fibre

PORK

smoky sticky pork ribs with coleslaw

PREP + COOK TIME 4¾ HOURS SERVES 4

2kg (4 pounds) american-style pork ribs
3 cloves garlic, crushed
1 cup (280g) barbecue sauce
¼ cup (60ml) lemon juice
¼ cup (55g) brown sugar
2 teaspoons sweet smoked paprika
1 teaspoon Tabasco sauce

CHEESY COLESLAW
¼ small green cabbage (300g)
¼ small red cabbage (300g)
1 large carrot (180g)
½ small red onion (50g)
1 cup (120g) coarsely grated vintage cheddar cheese
2 tablespoons coarsely chopped fresh chives
¾ cup (225g) mayonnaise
¼ cup (60ml) cider vinegar

1 Cut pork ribs into pieces that will fit into the slow cooker.
2 Combine garlic and the remaining ingredients in a large shallow dish; add pork, turn to coat pork in the marinade. Transfer pork and marinade to a 4.5-litre (18-cup) slow cooker. Cook, covered, on high, for 4 hours. Turn ribs once during cooking time for even cooking.
3 When almost ready to serve, make the cheesy coleslaw.
4 Carefully remove ribs from the cooker; cover to keep warm. Transfer sauce to a medium frying pan; bring to the boil. Reduce heat; simmer, uncovered, skimming fat from surface, for about 10 minutes or until sauce has reduced to 1 cup.
5 Drizzle pork with sauce. Serve with coleslaw.

CHEESY COLESLAW Finely shred cabbages. Coarsely grate carrot, and thinly slice the onion. Combine the cheese, chives, mayonnaise, vinegar, cabbage, carrot and onion in a large bowl; toss gently to combine. Season to taste.

Not suitable to freeze.

test kitchen tip

Ask the butcher to cut the ribs into pieces that will fit into your slow cooker.

nutritional count per serving
- 57.1g total fat
- 19.7g saturated fat
- 4592kJ (1097 cal)
- 64g carbohydrate
- 80g protein
- 6.9g fibre

pork with prunes

PREP + COOK TIME 9 HOURS SERVES 8

2kg (4-pound) boned pork shoulder

1½ tablespoons olive oil

500g (1 pound) pitted prunes

2 medium brown onions (300g), chopped finely

3 sprigs fresh thyme

3 cloves garlic, chopped finely

½ cup (125ml) port

½ cup (125ml) chicken stock

1 Season pork generously with salt and pepper
2 Heat 2 teaspoons of the oil in a large frying pan over medium-high heat; cook pork, turning, until browned all over. Transfer to a 4.5-litre (18-cup) slow cooker, then add prunes.
3 Heat remaining oil in the same pan over medium heat; cook onion and thyme, stirring, for 5 minutes or until onion softens. Stir in garlic; cook, stirring, for 1 minute or until fragrant.
4 Add port and stock to pan, stir to combine. Bring to the boil, then pour over pork. Cook, covered, on low, for 8 hours.

PORK

test kitchen tips

Sprinkle the prunes over the pork when adding to the cooker. This way they will have a better chance of staying whole if they're not squashed under the pork.

You can use either a tawny or ruby port for this recipe. Sherry will add a different flavour, but would also work well.

5 Carefully remove pork and half the prunes (preferably the whole ones); cover to keep warm. Strain cooking liquid into a large bowl; reserve solids, but discard thyme. Blend or process solids until smooth. Stir pureed onion mixture into cooking liquid until sauce thickens (you may not need to use all the onion mixture).
6 Slice pork; drizzle sauce over pork, serve with prunes.

serving suggestion Steamed broccoli and mashed potatoes or parsnip.

Suitable to freeze at the end of step 5.

nutritional count per serving
▶ 6.6g total fat
▶ 1.6g saturated fat
▶ 1823kJ (435 cal)
▶ 31.4g carbohydrate
▶ 57g protein
▶ 1.1g fibre

PORK

five-spice caramel pork belly

PREP + COOK TIME 7 HOURS SERVES 6

2kg (4-pound) boned pork belly, rind removed

2 litres (8 cups) water

1 cup (250ml) coconut water

1 cup (250ml) water, extra

¾ cup (180ml) fish sauce

½ cup (110g) firmly packed brown sugar

2 teaspoons five-spice powder

16 garlic cloves, unpeeled

6 eggs, at room temperature

6 fresh small thai red (serrano) chillies

¼ cup fresh coriander (cilantro) sprigs

CARAMEL

1 cup (220g) caster (superfine) sugar

½ cup (125ml) water

1 Cut pork into 4cm (1½-inch) pieces.
2 Place pork and the water in a large saucepan, bring to the boil over medium heat. Boil 5 minutes, skimming impurities from the surface; drain.
3 Meanwhile, make caramel.
4 Place pork in a 4.5-litre (18-cup) slow cooker with caramel, coconut water, the extra water, sauce, sugar, five spice and unpeeled garlic cloves. Cook, covered, on low, for 6 hours.
5 Meanwhile, place eggs in a medium saucepan; cover with cold water. Bring to the boil; boil eggs 6 minutes or until hard-boiled. Transfer to a bowl of cold water and cool slightly before peeling.
6 Add eggs and chillies to cooker. Cook, uncovered, on high, for 30 minutes; skim fat from surface. Sprinkle with coriander before serving.

CARAMEL Combine sugar and the water in a small saucepan; stir over high heat, without boiling, until sugar dissolves. Bring to the boil. Boil, uncovered, without stirring, until a deep golden caramel.

serving suggestion Steamed jasmine rice.

Suitable to freeze at the end of step 4.

nutritional count per serving
▶ 33.8g total fat
▶ 12.7g saturated fat
▶ 3550kJ (848 cal)
▶ 59.4g carbohydrate
▶ 78.3g protein
▶ 2g fibre

test kitchen tip

Coconut water is the liquid from the centre of an immature coconut. It is readily available in tetra packs and cans from a variety of supermarkets. Ensure it's labelled 100 per cent coconut water, and that it is not sweetened.

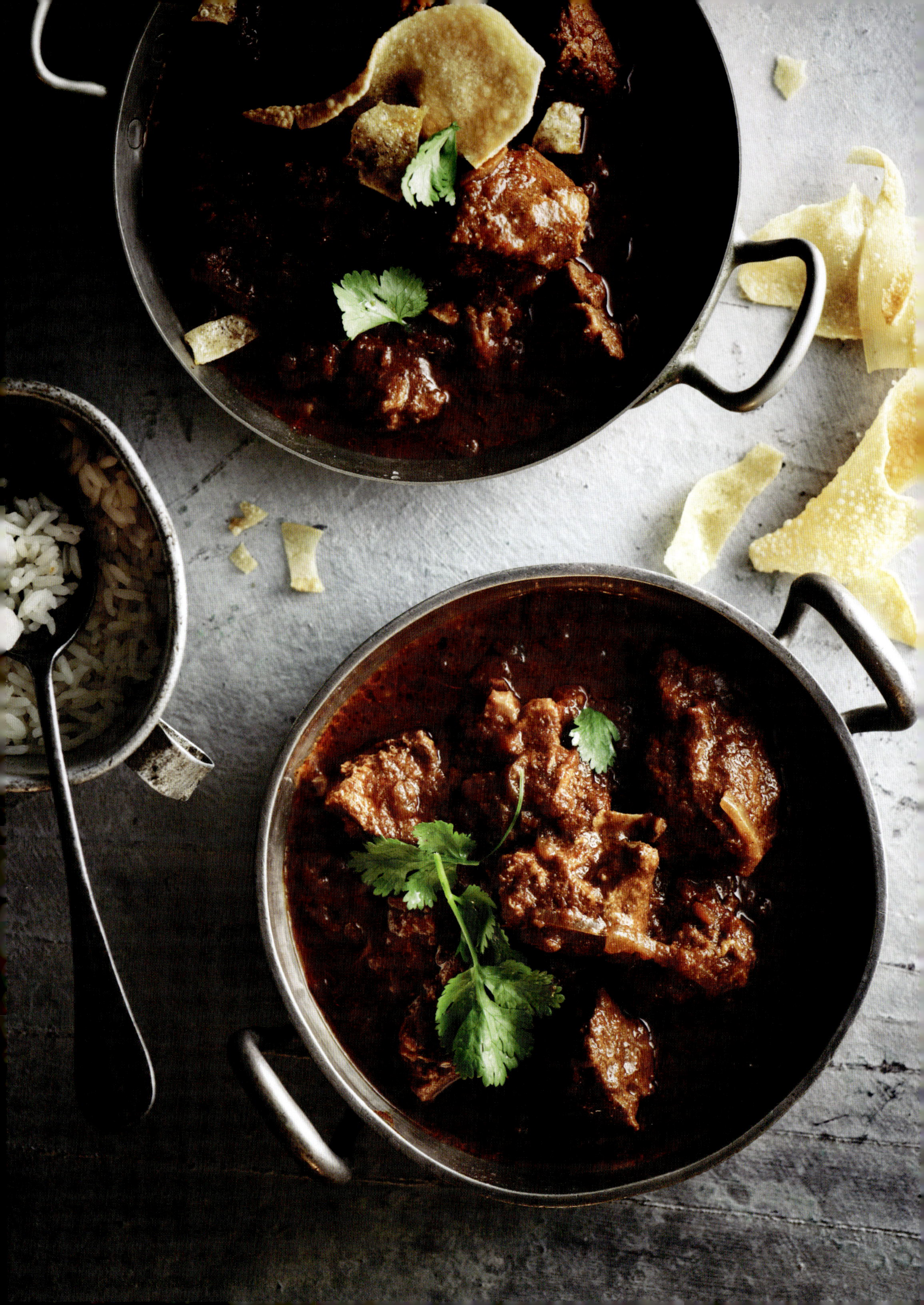

PORK

The king of curries, the fiery Indian vindaloo, is from the former Portuguese colony of Goa. The name is derived from the Portuguese words for vinegar and garlic, the dish's primary ingredients, which gives the dish its sweet/sour taste. Jars of vindaloo paste are available from supermarkets.

pork vindaloo

PREP + COOK TIME 8½ HOURS   SERVES 6

1.2kg (2½-pound) pork scotch fillet (neck)

2 large brown onions (400g), sliced thinly

5cm (2-inch) piece fresh ginger (25g), grated

2 cloves garlic, grated

400g (12½ ounces) canned diced tomatoes

½ cup (150g) vindaloo paste

2 tablespoons tomato paste

¾ cup (180ml) beef stock

½ cup loosely packed fresh coriander leaves (cilantro)

1 Cut pork into 3cm (1¼-inch) pieces; discard any excess fat.

2 Place pork, onion, ginger, garlic, tomatoes, the vindaloo and tomato pastes, and stock in a 4.5-litre (18-cup) slow cooker. Cook, covered, on low, for 8 hours. Sprinkle with coriander to serve.

serving suggestion Steamed basmati rice and pappadums.

Suitable to freeze without coriander.

nutritional count per serving
- 10.8g total fat
- 1.9g saturated fat
- 1406kJ (336 cal)
- 7.7g carbohydrate
- 49.1g protein
- 2.6g fibre

PORK

Most chilli spice mixes come as hot or mild; choose the heat level that you and your family can tolerate. Green chillies are chillies that are usually harvested when young and still green. As they ripen, their colour changes from green to red and the intensity of their flavour increases as well. The seeds and membranes contain the heat; removing them lessens the heat level.

pork and chilli stew

PREP + COOK TIME 8¾ HOURS SERVES 4

1 tablespoon olive oil

750g (1½ pounds) diced pork

1 medium red onion (170g), chopped finely

2 cloves garlic, chopped finely

1 medium red capsicum (bell pepper) (200g), chopped coarsely

500g (1 pound) baby new potatoes, quartered

35g (1-ounce) sachet chilli spice mix

400g (12½ ounces) canned corn kernels, rinsed, drained

800g (1½ pounds) canned diced tomatoes

2 limes

½ cup (140g) sour cream

2 fresh long green chillies, sliced thinly

¼ cup chopped fresh coriander (cilantro)

1 Heat oil in a large frying pan over medium-high heat; cook pork, turning, until browned. Transfer to a 4.5-litre (18-cup) slow cooker.
2 Place onion, garlic, capsicum, potato, spice mix, corn kernels and tomatoes in the cooker. Cook, covered, on low, for 8 hours.
3 Cut cheeks from limes. Divide pork mixture among serving bowls. Top with sour cream, chilli and coriander; accompany with lime cheeks.

serving suggestion Accompany with tortilla chips.

Suitable to freeze at the end of step 2.

nutritional count per serving
▶ 25.1g total fat
▶ 12.2g saturated fat
▶ 2579kJ (616 cal)
▶ 42.8g carbohydrate
▶ 49.1g protein
▶ 8.5g fibre

test kitchen tip
If the potatoes are very small, halve them rather than cutting them into quarters.

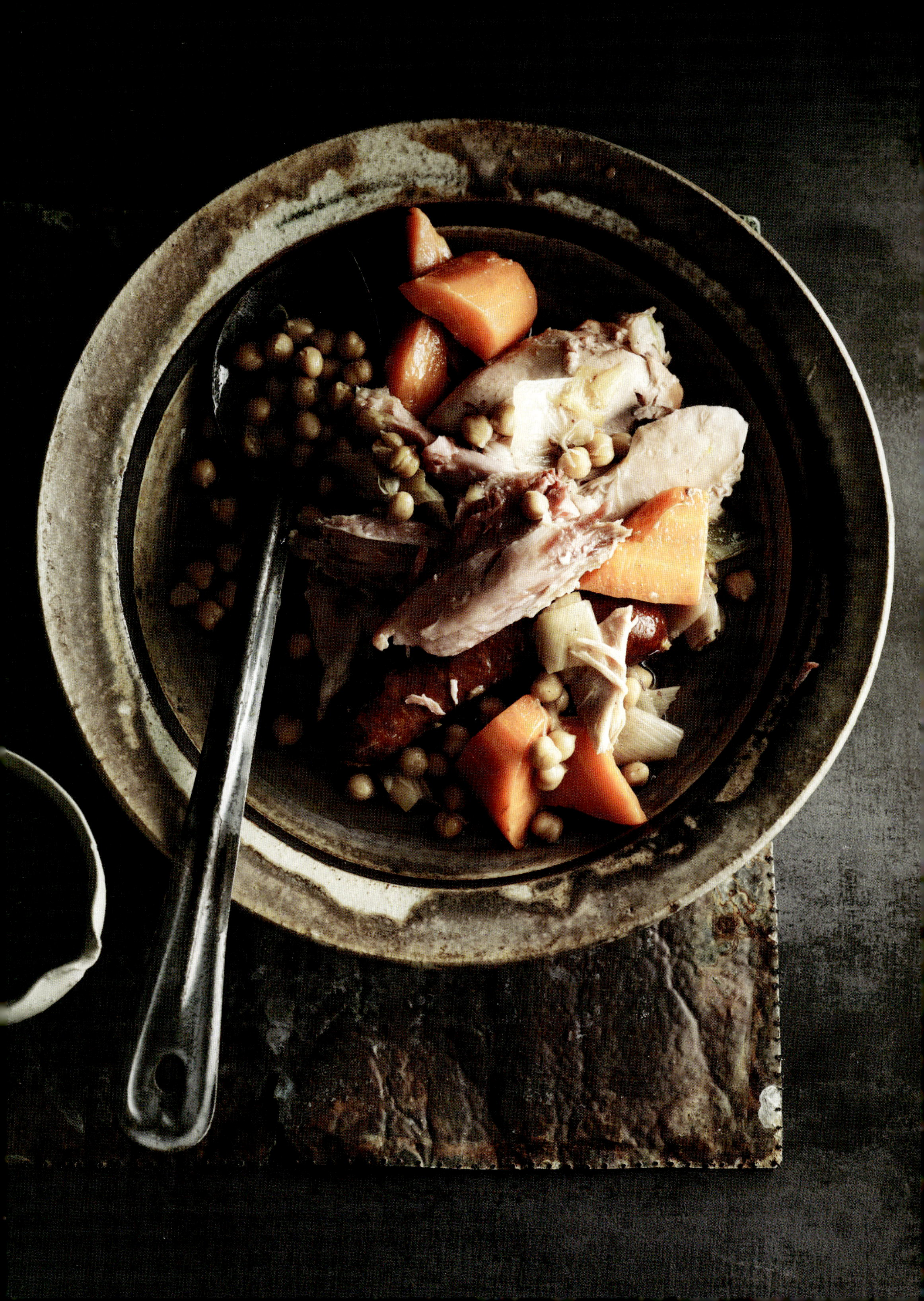

PORK

Pronounced 'co-see-do', this is a traditional Spanish chickpea and meat-based stew.

spanish cocido

PREP + COOK TIME 8½ HOURS SERVES 4

2 medium leeks (700g), chopped coarsely
2 large carrots (360g), chopped coarsely
pinch saffron threads
1 bay leaf
2 x 400g (12½-ounce) cans chickpeas (garbanzo beans), rinsed, drained
350g (11 ounces) beef chuck steak
1 raw chorizo (170g)
1kg (2-pound) meaty ham hock
2 chicken thigh cutlets (400g)
1 litre (4 cups) water

1 Place leek, carrot, saffron, bay leaf, chickpeas, beef, chorizo, ham hock and chicken in a 4.5-litre (18-cup) slow cooker. Pour over the water. Cook, covered, on low, for 8 hours.
2 Remove ham and chicken from bones in large chunks; divide among bowls with chorizo, beef, vegetables and chickpeas.

serving suggestion Accompany with crusty bread to soak up the broth.

Suitable to freeze at the end of step 2.

test kitchen tips

Ask the butcher to chop the end off the ham hock where there's no meat. The broth is often served first, as a starter, with rice and noodles, but you can also serve the meat and vegetables with some broth in shallow bowls.

nutritional count per serving
▶ 16.9g total fat
▶ 5.2g saturated fat
▶ 2032kJ (485 cal)
▶ 26g carbohydrate
▶ 52.2g protein
▶ 11.7g fibre

PORK

sweet and sour italian pork with capsicum

PREP + COOK TIME 8¾ HOURS SERVES 6

1.5kg (3-pound) piece pork scotch fillet (neck)
2 tablespoons olive oil
2 medium red capsicums (bell peppers) (400g)
2 medium brown onions (300g) chopped finely
1 stalk celery (150g), trimmed, chopped coarsely
2 cloves garlic, chopped finely
¼ cup (55g) caster (superfine) sugar
½ cup (125ml) red wine vinegar
2 tablespoons tomato paste
½ cup (125ml) chicken stock
¼ cup (40g) sultanas
2 tablespoons pine nuts
2 tablespoons chopped fresh flat-leaf parsley

1 Tie the pork with kitchen string at 2cm (¾-inch) intervals. Heat half the oil in a large frying pan over medium-high heat; cook the pork until browned. Transfer to a 4.5-litre (18-cup) slow cooker.
2 Meanwhile, cut capsicums lengthways into eighths; discard seeds and membranes.
3 Heat remaining oil in same pan over medium heat; cook onion, celery and garlic, stirring occasionally, for 5 minutes or until softened. Add sugar; cook, stirring occasionally, about 10 minutes or until golden and caramelised. Add vinegar to the pan; bring to the boil. Stir in paste and stock; bring to the boil, then pour over pork. Add sultanas and capsicum to the cooker.
4 Cook, covered, on low, for 8 hours. Carefully remove pork from cooker; transfer to serving plate, cover to keep warm.
5 Meanwhile, toast nuts in a dry frying pan, stirring continuously over medium heat until just golden. Remove immediately from pan. Spoon sauce over pork. Serve sprinkled with nuts and parsley.

serving suggestion Serve with mashed potato or polenta.

Suitable to freeze at the end of step 4.

nutritional count per serving
▶ 10.7g total fat
▶ 2.2g saturated fat
▶ 1789kJ (427 cal)
▶ 19.3g carbohydrate
▶ 61.1g protein
▶ 3.2g fibre

'Agrodolce' is the Italian word used to describe the flavours in this dish and means 'sour sweet'.

test kitchen tip
Make sure the ham hocks are not too large to fit in the slow cooker. Ask the butcher to cut them for you, if necessary.

PORK

ham and green lentil soup with gremolata

PREP + COOK TIME 8½ HOURS   SERVES 6

1.8kg (3½-pounds) meaty ham hocks
½ cup (100g) french-style green lentils
1 tablespoon vegetable oil
2 medium brown onions (300g), chopped finely
2 medium carrots (240g), chopped finely
2 stalks celery (300g), trimmed, chopped finely
1 teaspoon fresh thyme leaves
2 cups (500ml) salt-reduced chicken stock
1.5 litres (6 cups) water

GREMOLATA
2 cloves garlic, crushed
¼ cup finely chopped fresh flat-leaf parsley
2 teaspoons finely grated lemon rind

1 Rinse ham hocks. Place in a 4.5-litre (18-cup) slow cooker.
2 Rinse lentils; drain well.
3 Heat oil in a medium frying pan over medium heat; cook onion, stirring, for 5 minutes or until softened. Transfer onion to the cooker with carrot, celery, thyme, lentils, stock and the water.
4 Cook, covered, on low, for 8 hours. Carefully remove hock from cooker. When cool enough to handle, remove and discard skin and bones. Shred meat finely using two forks. Return meat to cooker. Season to taste.
5 When almost ready to serve, make gremolata; sprinkle over soup to serve.

GREMOLATA Combine ingredients in a small bowl.

serving suggestion Accompany with crusty bread.

Suitable to freeze at the end of step 4.

nutritional count per serving
▶ 10.3g total fat
▶ 2.8g saturated fat
▶ 1108kJ (265 cal)
▶ 12g carbohydrate
▶ 28.6g protein
▶ 5.4g fibre

VEGETABLES

stuffed capsicums

PREP + COOK TIME 3¾ HOURS **MAKES** 5

2 tablespoons olive oil
1 medium brown onion (150g), chopped finely
3 cloves garlic, crushed
2 tablespoons tomato paste
1 cup (280g) bottled passata
¾ cup (150g) quinoa
1 cup (250ml) chicken stock
400g (12½ ounces) canned brown lentils, rinsed, drained
180g (5½ ounces) greek fetta cheese, crumbled
⅓ cup (50g) pitted black olives, finely chopped
¼ cup coarsely chopped fresh flat-leaf parsley
¼ cup coarsely chopped fresh basil
5 medium capsicums (1kg)

1 Heat oil in a large frying pan over medium heat; cook onion and garlic, stirring, for 5 minutes or until onion softens. Add paste, passata, quinoa and stock; bring to the boil. Remove from heat. Stir in lentils, cheese, olives and herbs. Season to taste.
2 Cut tops from each capsicum; reserve tops. Using a small spoon, scoop out the membranes and seeds. Trim bases level so that the capsicums stand upright in the slow cooker. Divide quinoa mixture among the capsicums; replace the tops.
3 Place the capsicums into a 4.5-litre (18-cup) slow cooker. Cook, covered, on high, for 3 hours.

serving suggestion Accompany with greek-style yoghurt.

Not suitable to freeze.

nutritional count per serving
- 15.4g total fat
- 7.6g saturated fat
- 1638kJ (391 cal)
- 39g carbohydrate
- 20.6g protein
- 7.9g fibre

test kitchen tips

Choose capsicums that are taller rather than wider, so they all fit into the slow cooker. Passata is sieved tomato puree; it is available from supermarkets.

Quinoa, pronounced 'keen-wa', is the seed of a leafy plant similar to spinach. It has a delicate, slightly nutty taste and chewy texture. It is available from most supermarkets and health-food stores.

cheese, tomato and olive bread pudding

PREP + COOK TIME 3½ HOURS SERVES 6

- 40g (1½ ounces) butter, softened
- 6 green onions (scallions), trimmed, sliced thinly
- 2 cloves garlic, crushed
- 6 x 1.5cm (¾-inch) thick slices olive bread (360g)
- ½ cup (80g) pitted black olives, halved
- 200g (6½ ounces) cherry tomatoes
- ½ cup (40g) finely grated parmesan cheese
- 100g (3 ounces) drained persian fetta cheese
- 1 tablespoon coarsely chopped fresh basil
- 6 eggs
- 1 cup (250ml) milk
- 300ml (½ pint) reduced-fat thickened (heavy) cream
- ¼ teaspoon sweet paprika

VEGETABLES

nutritional count per serving
▶ 32.6g total fat
▶ 16.5g saturated fat
▶ 2071kJ (495 cal)
▶ 29g carbohydrate
▶ 20.3g protein
▶ 3.1g fibre

1 Grease a 4.5-litre (18-cup) slow cooker bowl with a little of the butter.
2 Heat 20g (¾ ounce) of the butter in a small frying pan; cook onion and garlic, stirring, for 5 minutes or until softened.
3 Spread bread with remaining butter; cut each slice in half. Place half the bread in the base of the cooker. Sprinkle half the onion mixture over bread; layer with half the of tomatoes, olives, parmesan, crumbled fetta and basil. Season to taste. Repeat with remaining bread, onion mixture, tomatoes, olives, cheese and basil.
4 Whisk eggs, milk and cream together in a large jug; season. Pour egg mixture over bread mixture. Sprinkle with paprika.
5 Cook, covered, on low, for about 3 hours or until set. Remove bowl from cooker. Stand for 5 minutes before serving, scattered with baby basil and parmesan cheese, if you like.

serving suggestion Leafy green salad.

Not suitable to freeze.

VEGETABLES

parmesan, spinach and bean ragù

PREP + COOK TIME 8¾ HOURS SERVES 6

375g (12 ounces) dried four-bean mix
50g (1½ ounces) butter, chopped coarsely
1 tablespoon olive oil
1 large brown onion (200g), chopped finely
1 medium carrot (120g), chopped finely
2 stalks celery (300g), trimmed, chopped finely
3 cloves garlic, crushed
½ cup (125ml) dry white wine
2 tablespoons tomato paste
400g (12½ ounces) canned crushed tomatoes
2 cups (500ml) vegetable stock
2 teaspoons sea salt flakes
2 teaspoons caster (superfine) sugar
4 sprigs fresh thyme
50g (1½ ounces) baby spinach leaves
1 cup (80g) finely grated parmesan cheese

1 Place bean mix in a medium saucepan; cover with 5cm (2-inches) cold water. Bring to the boil over a medium-low heat. Boil for 5 minutes; drain. Transfer beans to a 4.5-litre (18-cup) slow cooker.
2 Heat butter and oil in a large frying pan over medium heat; cook onion, carrot, celery and garlic, stirring, for 5 minutes or until softened. Add wine; bring to the boil. Boil until the wine has almost evaporated. Add paste, tomatoes, stock, salt, sugar and thyme. Transfer to the cooker. Cook, covered, on low, for 8 hours. Season to taste.
3 Discard thyme. Stir in spinach until wilted. Sprinkle ragù with parmesan to serve.

serving suggestion Accompany with fresh crusty bread.
tip We used a chardonnay-style wine in this recipe.

Not suitable to freeze.

nutritional count per serving
▶ 12.8g total fat
▶ 7.4g saturated fat
▶ 1093kJ (261 cal)
▶ 19.4g carbohydrate
▶ 12.8g protein
▶ 7g fibre

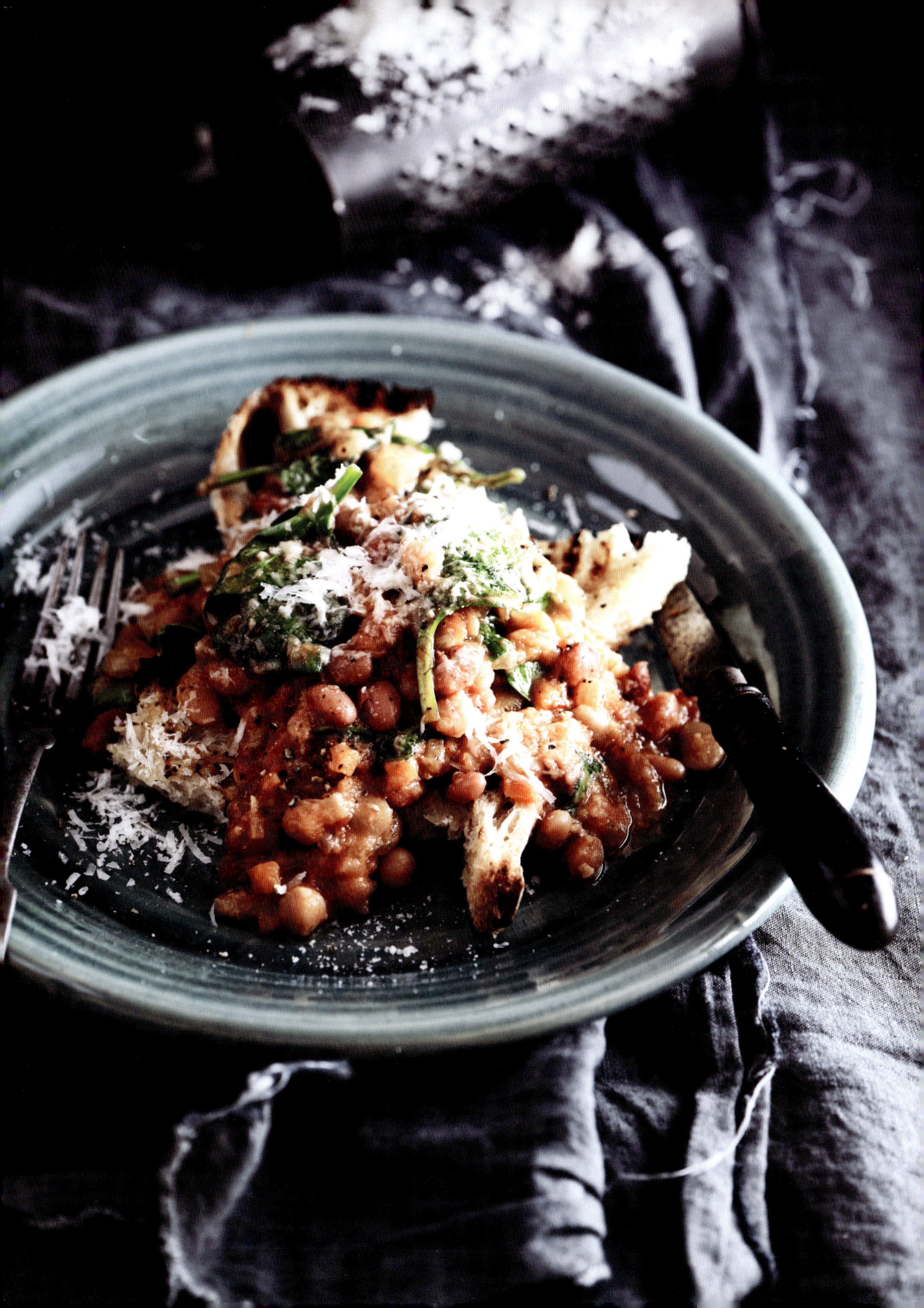

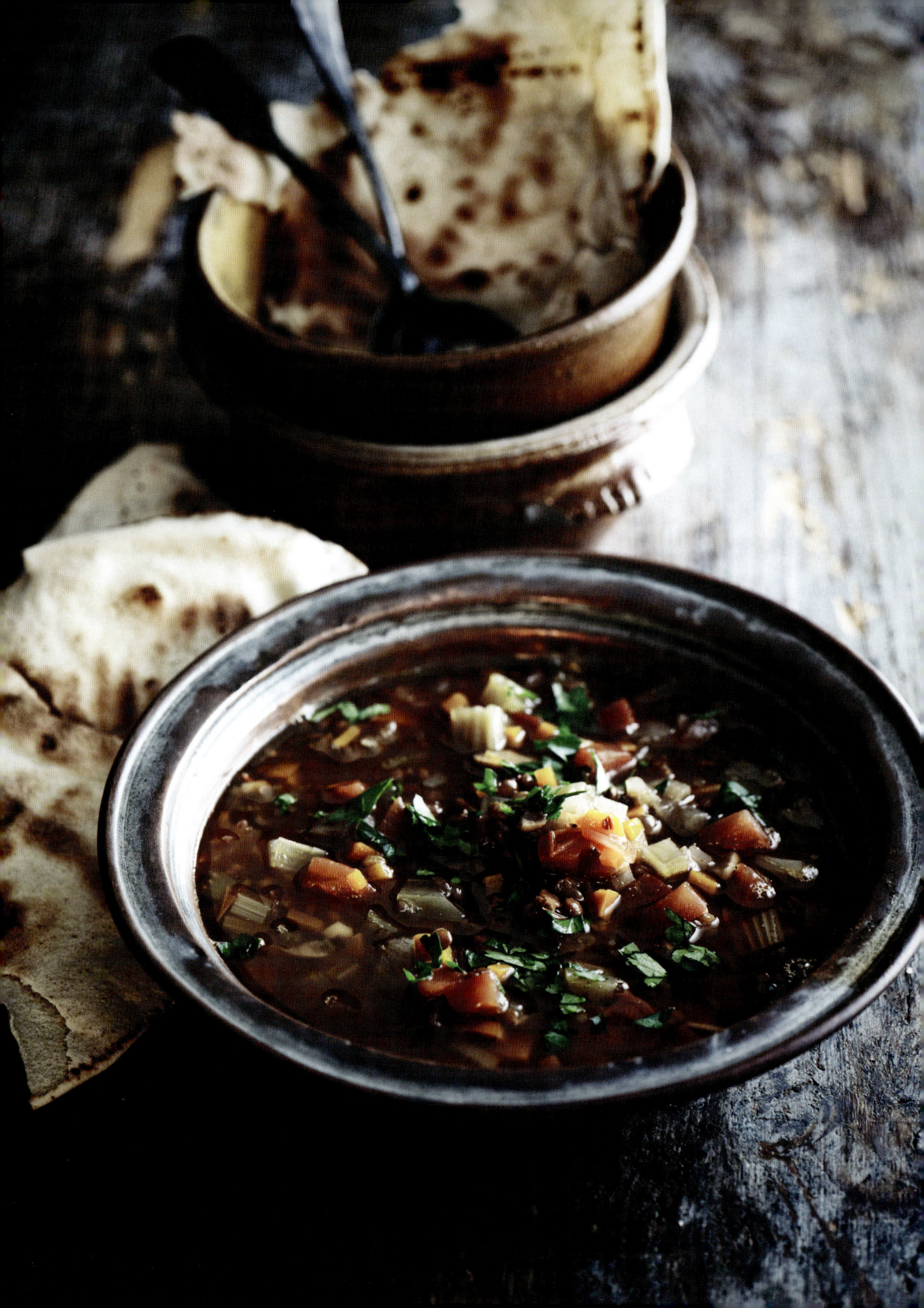

VEGETABLES

Harira is a traditional soup that's eaten to break the fast of Ramadan. This is our vegetarian version, but lamb, chicken or beef can be added.

vegetable harira

PREP + COOK TIME 8¾ HOURS SERVES 8

2 teaspoons each ground cumin, coriander and sweet smoked paprika
1 teaspoon each ground ginger, cinnamon and dried chilli flakes
¼ teaspoon ground nutmeg
1 large brown onion (200g), chopped finely
2 medium carrots (240g), chopped finely
4 stalks celery (600g), trimmed, chopped finely
5 medium tomatoes (750g), chopped finely
6 cloves garlic, crushed
2 tablespoons tomato paste
1.5 litres (6 cups) vegetable stock
1 litre (4 cups) water
1 cup (200g) french-style green lentils
400g (12½ ounces) canned chickpeas (garbanzo beans), rinsed, drained
⅓ cup each finely chopped fresh flat-leaf parsley and coriander (cilantro)

1 Dry-fry spices in a small frying pan over medium heat for 1 minute or until fragrant.

2 Combine onion, carrot, celery, tomato, garlic, spices, paste, stock, the water and lentils in a 4.5-litre (18-cup) slow cooker. Cook, covered, on low, for 8 hours. Season to taste.

3 Add chickpeas to cooker and stir until heated through. Stir in parsley and coriander to serve.

serving suggestion Accompany with lemon wedges and warm flat bread; drizzle over extra virgin olive oil.

Not suitable to freeze.

---

nutritional count per serving
- 2.6g total fat
- 0.4g saturated fat
- 753kJ (180 cal)
- 23.1g carbohydrate
- 12g protein
- 9.4g fibre

VEGETABLES

Cannelloni are large pasta tubes usually stuffed with a meat or cheese filling and baked. The name is also used for the finished dish. Firm ricotta cheese is available from supermarket delicatessens and cheese shops. It is not the same as the soft ricotta found in tubs in the dairy section.

spinach and three cheese cannelloni

PREP + COOK TIME 5 HOURS   SERVES 6

750g (1½ pounds) frozen spinach, thawed

3½ cups (840g) firm ricotta cheese

2 eggs

1 egg yolk

¾ cup (60g) finely grated parmesan cheese

225g (7 ounces) jar char-grilled eggplant in olive oil, drained, chopped finely

3 cloves garlic, crushed

1 litre (4 cups) bottled passata

¾ cup (180ml) pouring cream

¾ cup coarsely chopped fresh basil

400g (12½ ounces) dried instant cannelloni tubes

1½ cups (180g) pizza cheese

1 Squeeze excess moisture from the spinach. Place spinach, ricotta, eggs, egg yolk, parmesan, eggplant and garlic in a large bowl; stir to combine. Season.
2 Combine passata, cream and basil in a large jug; season.
3 Lightly oil a 4.5-litre (18-cup) slow cooker. Pour half the passata mixture over base of the cooker.
4 Spoon or pipe spinach mixture into cannelloni tubes; arrange cannelloni vertically in cooker. Top with remaining passata mixture; sprinkle with pizza cheese. Cook, covered, on low, for 4 hours. Stand for 10 minutes before serving.

serving suggestion Accompany with extra basil leaves and parmesan cheese.
tip Passata is sieved tomato puree available from supermarkets.

Not suitable to freeze.

nutritional count per serving
- 41.8g total fat
- 24.7g saturated fat
- 3493kJ (834 cal)
- 66.6g carbohydrate
- 45.3g protein
- 3.4g fibre

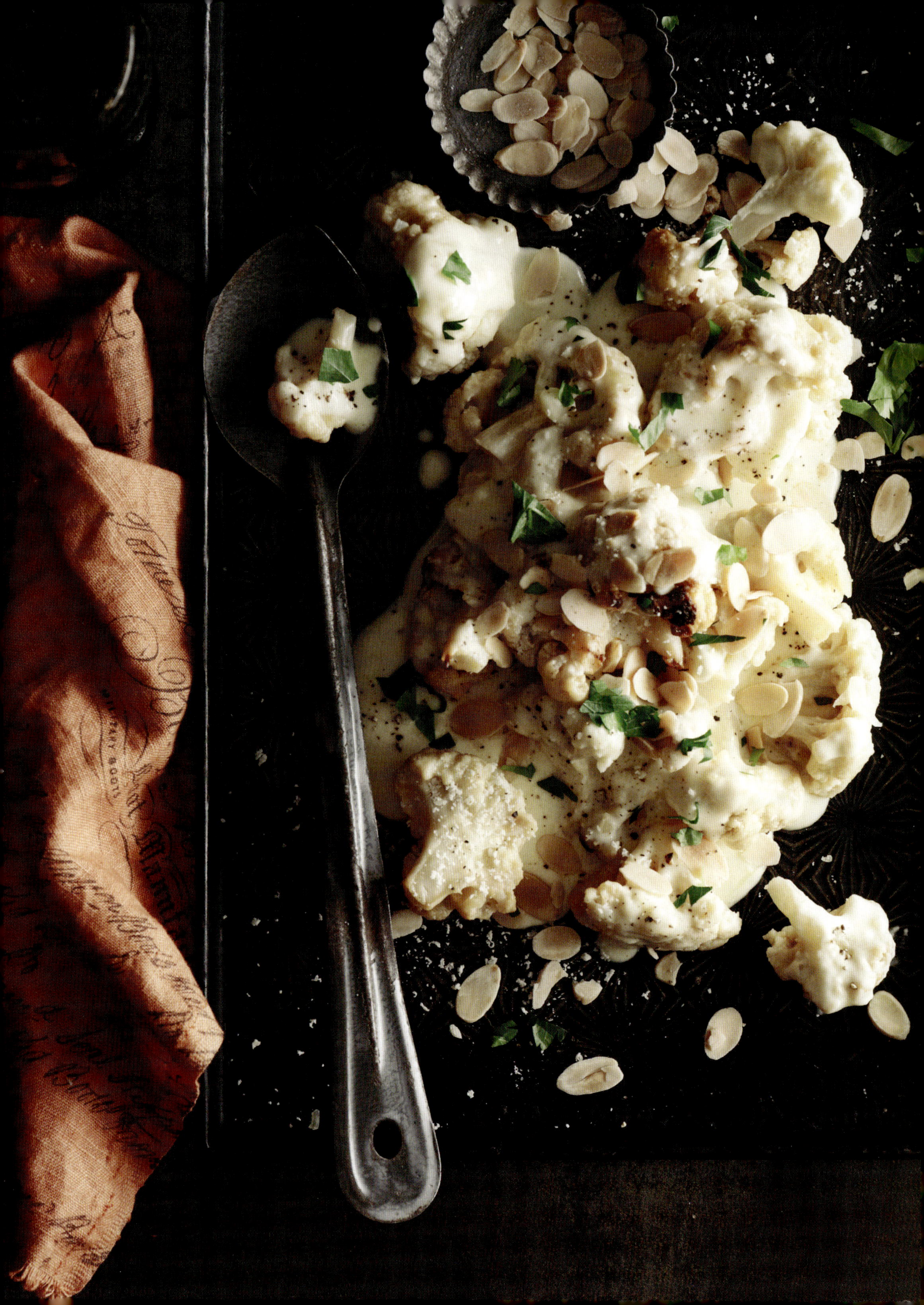

cauliflower cheese

PREP + COOK TIME 3½ HOURS SERVES 6

50g (1½ ounces) butter, chopped coarsely
2 tablespoons plain (all-purpose) flour
2 cups (500ml) milk
1¼ cups (150g) grated swiss cheese
1 medium cauliflower (1.5kg), cut into florets
1 medium brown onion (150g), chopped finely
½ cup (40g) finely grated parmesan cheese
⅓ cup (25g) flaked almonds
¼ cup coarsely chopped fresh flat-leaf parsley

1 Melt butter in a medium saucepan over medium heat, add flour; cook, stirring, for about 2 minutes or until mixture thickens and bubbles. Gradually stir in milk; cook, stirring, until sauce boils and thickens. Remove from heat; stir in swiss cheese until melted.

2 Place cauliflower and onion into a 4.5-litre (18-cup) slow cooker; toss to combine. Season to taste. Pour over cheese sauce; toss to coat. Sprinkle with parmesan.

3 Cook, covered, on low, for 3 hours. Sprinkle with nuts and parsley to serve.

serving suggestion Pan-fried steaks or chicken breasts.

Not suitable to freeze.

---

nutritional count per serving
- 22.5g total fat
- 12.8g saturated fat
- 1421kJ (339 cal)
- 12.3g carbohydrate
- 18.9g protein
- 7.2g fibre

VEGETABLES

Serve this chunky-style sauce over 500g (1 pound) cooked short tubular pasta – both casarecce and penne pasta work well.

eggplant, olive and pine nut pasta sauce

PREP + COOK TIME 6½ HOURS SERVES 6

3 cloves garlic, chopped finely
2 medium brown onions (300g), chopped finely
1 fresh long red chilli, chopped finely
500g (1 pound) ripe tomatoes, chopped coarsely
1 large eggplant (500g), chopped coarsely
400g (12½ ounces) canned diced tomatoes
½ cup lightly packed fresh basil leaves
2 tablespoons tomato paste
½ cup (75g) pitted black olives
2 tablespoons toasted pine nuts
⅓ cup finely shredded fresh basil leaves

1 Place garlic, onion, chilli, fresh tomato, eggplant, canned tomatoes, basil leaves (reserve a few of the smallest to serve) and paste in a 4.5-litre (18-cup) slow cooker; stir to combine.
2 Cook, covered, on low, for 6 hours. Season to taste.
3 Add olives, nuts and shredded basil to cooker; stir to combine. Sprinkle reserved small basil leaves over sauce before serving.

Not suitable to freeze.

nutritional count per serving
▶ 6.5g total fat
▶ 0.5g saturated fat
▶ 534kJ (128 cal)
▶ 9.7g carbohydrate
▶ 4.2g protein
▶ 6.4g fibre

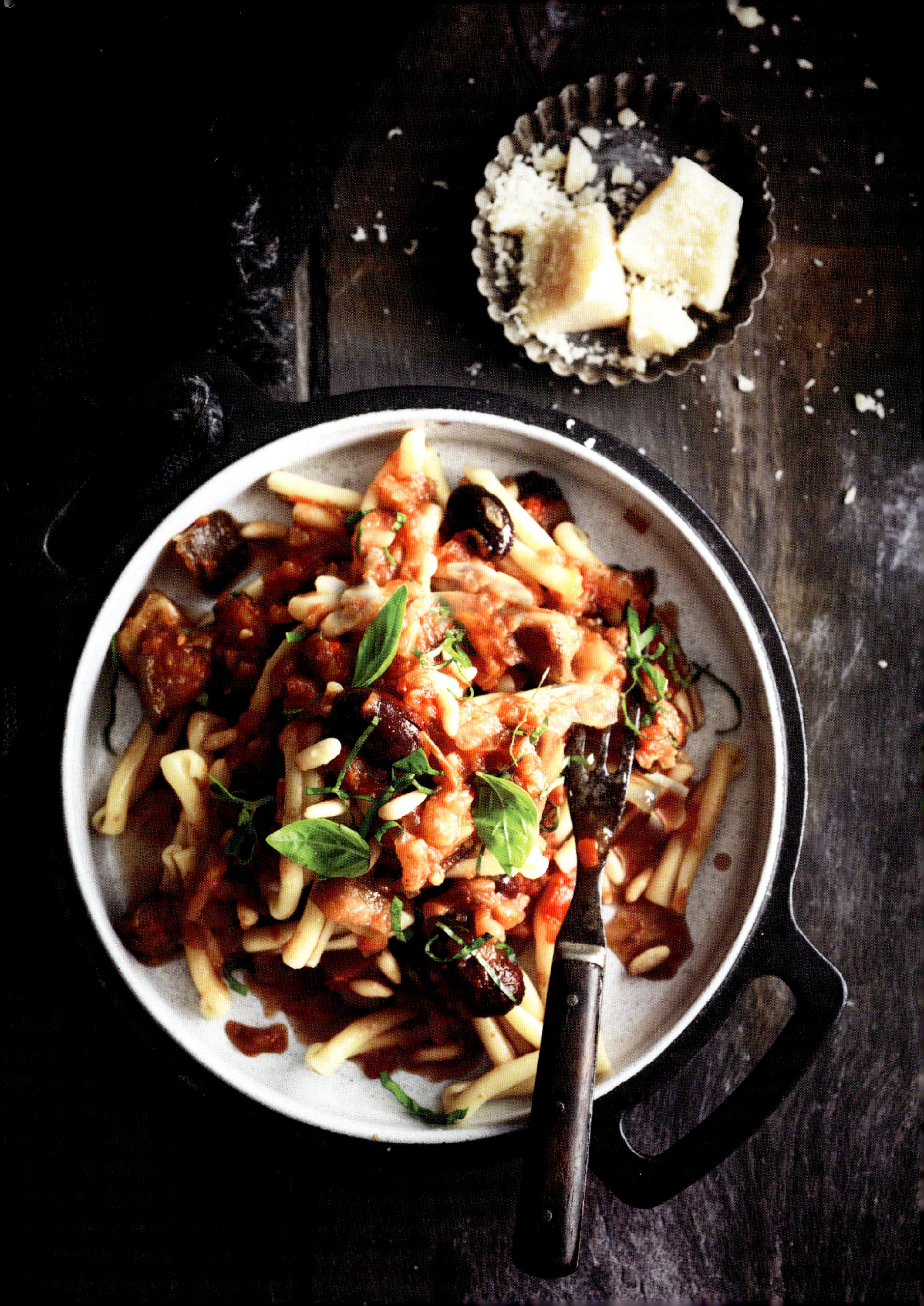

nutritional count per serving
- 8.7g total fat
- 3.8g saturated fat
- 1113kJ (266 cal)
- 29.9g carbohydrate
- 12.3g protein
- 10.6g fibre

VEGETABLES

Choose the ripest tomatoes you can find. If you dislike tomato skins, you can either peel the tomatoes before adding to the cooker or strain the pureed soup before returning the chickpeas.

smoky chickpea and tomato soup

PREP + COOK TIME 8½ HOURS SERVES 6

1.5kg (3 pounds) tomatoes, quartered
1 large brown onion (200g), chopped coarsely
3 cloves garlic, chopped coarsely
1 stalk celery (150g), trimmed, sliced thickly
3 x 400g (12½-ounce) cans chickpeas (garbanzo beans), rinsed, drained
1¾ cups (430ml) chicken stock
2 teaspoons smoked paprika
1 tablespoon caster (superfine) sugar
⅓ cup (80g) sour cream

1 Place tomato, onion, garlic, celery, chickpeas, stock, paprika and sugar in a 4.5-litre (18-cup) slow cooker. Cook, covered, on low, for 8 hours.
2 Using a slotted spoon, transfer 2 cups of chickpeas to a medium bowl; reserve. Stand remaining soup 10 minutes, then process soup until smooth. Stir in reserved chickpeas. Season to taste.
3 Serve soup topped with sour cream.

serving suggestion Accompany with char-grilled bread slices.

Suitable to freeze at the end of step 3.

VEGETABLES

pumpkin, sage and zucchini lasagne

PREP + COOK TIME 4¾ HOURS SERVES 6

1kg (2 pounds) pumpkin, chopped coarsely
60g (2 ounces) butter, chopped
5 cloves garlic, crushed
1½ tablespoons finely chopped fresh sage
3 cups (720g) firm ricotta cheese
1 egg
¼ teaspoon ground nutmeg
1 cup (80g) finely grated parmesan cheese
3 medium zucchini (360g)
cooking-oil spray
⅓ cup (80ml) pouring cream
8 dried instant lasagne sheets (120g)
1 cup (100g) coarsely grated mozzarella cheese

1 Boil, steam or microwave pumpkin until tender; drain.
2 Melt butter in a large frying pan over medium heat; cook garlic and sage for 1 minute or until fragrant. Stir in pumpkin; remove from heat. Season.
3 Combine ricotta, egg, nutmeg and half the parmesan in a large bowl; season.
4 Thinly slice zucchini lengthways using a vegetable peeler.
5 Lightly spray a 4.5-litre (18-cup) slow cooker with oil. Drizzle 2 tablespoons of cream over base; top with 2 lasagne sheets, breaking to fit.
6 Spread one-third of the pumpkin mixture over pasta; top with one-third of the zucchini slices, then one-quarter of the ricotta mixture. Top with 2 more lasagne sheets. Repeat layering, finishing with pasta. Pour over the remaining cream, then spread with the remaining ricotta mixture. Sprinkle with mozzarella and remaining parmesan. Cook, covered, on low, for 4 hours or until pasta is tender.

serving suggestion Leafy green salad.

Suitable to freeze at the end of step 6.

nutritional count per serving
▶ 37.1g total fat
▶ 22.6g saturated fat
▶ 2377kJ (568 cal)
▶ 27.9g carbohydrate
▶ 28.9g protein
▶ 4.7g fibre

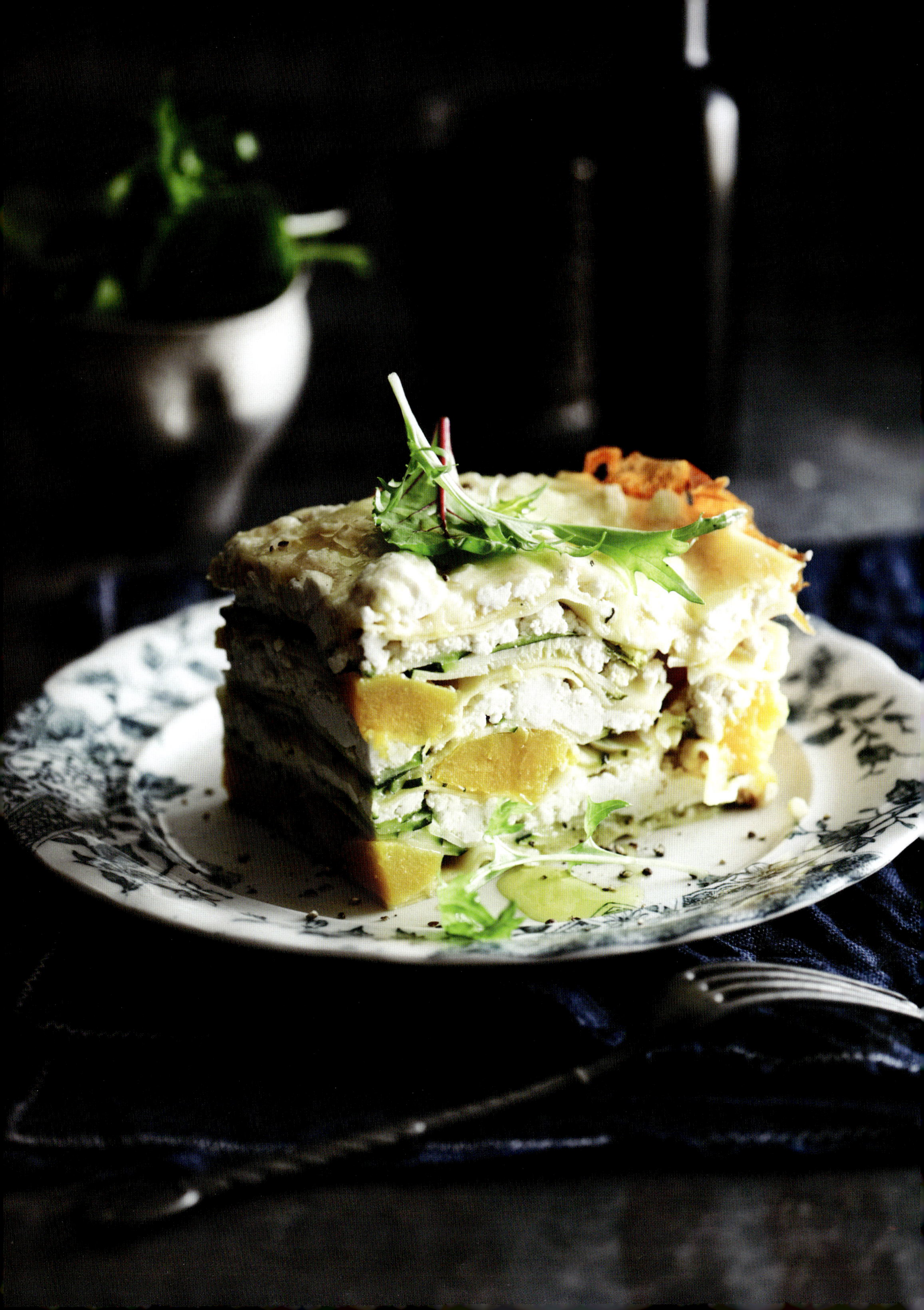

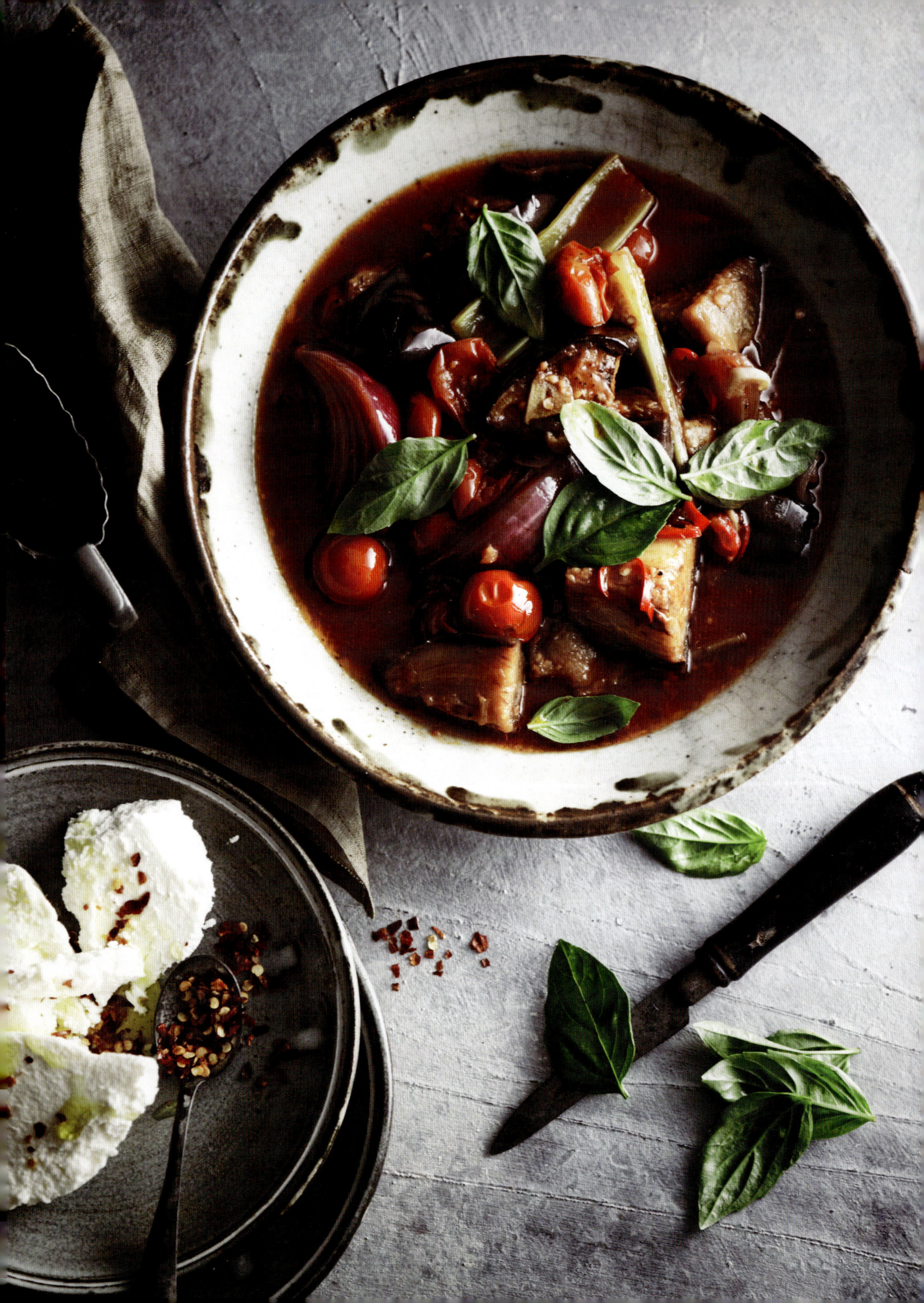

eggplant, chilli and tomato stew with ricotta

PREP + COOK TIME 2¾ HOURS SERVES 4

- 2 celery stalks (300g), trimmed
- 4 cloves garlic, sliced thinly
- 1 fresh long red chilli, sliced thinly
- 2 x 400g (12½-ounce) cans cherry tomatoes
- 2 medium red onions (340g), unpeeled
- ¼ cup (60ml) olive oil
- 2 medium eggplants (600g)
- 400g (12½-ounce) wedge fresh firm ricotta
- ½ teaspoon dried chilli flakes
- 2 teaspoons olive oil, extra
- ¼ cup lightly packed fresh basil leaves

1 Cut celery into 7.5cm (3-inch) lengths. Place garlic, chilli, celery and tomatoes in a 4.5-litre (18-cup) slow cooker. Season.
2 Peel onions leaving root end intact. Cut each onion into eight wedges.
3 Heat 1 tablespoon of oil in a medium frying pan over medium-high heat; cook onion, turning, until browned. Transfer to cooker.
4 Meanwhile, chop eggplant into 5cm (2-inch) pieces. Heat remaining oil in the same pan over medium heat; cook eggplant, turning occasionally, until browned. Transfer to cooker.
5 Cook, covered, on high, for 2 hours. Season to taste.
6 Cut ricotta into 4 wedges; place on serving platter. Sprinkle with chilli; drizzle with extra oil.
7 To serve, sprinkle eggplant stew with basil; accompany with ricotta wedges.

serving suggestion Soft polenta and grilled crusty bread.
tip Canned cherry tomatoes are available from most supermarkets. You can use canned chopped or diced tomatoes instead.

Not suitable to freeze.

nutritional count per serving
- 29.3g total fat
- 10g saturated fat
- 1603kJ (383 cal)
- 12.5g carbohydrate
- 14.4g protein
- 7.7g fibre

PUDDINGS

chocolate and cherry puddings

PREP + COOK TIME 1¾ HOURS MAKES 4

125g (4 ounces) butter, softened
¾ cup (165g) caster (superfine) sugar
1 teaspoon vanilla extract
2 eggs
¾ cup (110g) self-raising flour
½ cup (50g) dutch cocoa
¼ cup (60ml) milk
60g (2 ounces) dark (semi-sweet) chocolate, chopped finely
670g (15 ounces) pitted morello cherries in syrup, drained
⅓ cup (80ml) thick (double) cream

1 Grease four 1-cup (250ml) deep heatproof dishes.
2 Beat butter, sugar and extract in a small bowl with an electric mixer until light and fluffy. Beat in eggs, one at a time. Stir in the sifted dry ingredients then the milk and chocolate. Fold in half the cherries. Divide mixture between dishes.
3 Place dishes in a 4.5-litre (18-cup) slow cooker. Pour in enough boiling water to come halfway up the side of the dishes. Cook, covered, on high, for about 1½ hours or until mixture is firm. Remove puddings from cooker; dust with extra cocoa if you like and serve with cream and remaining cherries.

tip Ensure the four heatproof dishes fit into your slow cooker.

Not suitable to freeze.

nutritional count per serving
- 42.3g total fat
- 23.5g saturated fat
- 2971kJ (710 cal)
- 72.2g carbohydrate
- 10.1g protein
- 2.5g fibre

sago plum puddings

PREP + COOK TIME 4 HOURS (+ COOLING & REFRIGERATION) SERVES 4

You need to soak the sago overnight, so start the recipe the day before.

1 cup (250ml) milk

⅓ cup (65g) sago (seed tapioca)

1½ teaspoons bicarbonate of soda

40g (1½ ounces) butter, chopped

1 teaspoon finely grated orange rind

1 egg

½ cup (110g) caster (superfine) sugar

⅔ cup (110g) sultanas

1 cup (70g) stale breadcrumbs

1 Place the milk in a medium saucepan; bring to the boil then remove from heat. Stir in sago and soda (the mixture will foam). Transfer to a large bowl; cool to room temperature. Cover sago, refrigerate overnight.

2 Grease four ¾-cup (180ml) straight sided or fluted dariole moulds; line bases with baking paper. (Make sure the moulds fit in the cooker).

3 Melt butter. Add the butter, rind, egg, sugar, sultanas and breadcrumbs to sago mixture; stir to combine.

4 Spoon sago mixture into moulds. Cut out rounds of baking paper 2cm (¾-inch) larger than the top of the moulds. Make a vertical pleat down the centre of the paper; place paper over the moulds and secure with kitchen string.

Sago and tapioca, while similar, are not the same and can't be substituted for each other. Sago may be found labelled as 'seed tapioca' on some packets. It is available from most health-food stores and supermarkets.

5 Place moulds in a 4.5-litre (18-cup) slow cooker. Pour in enough boiling water to come halfway up the side of the moulds. Cook, covered, on high, for about 3½ hours or until mixture is firm to touch.
6 Remove puddings from cooker; stand for 5 minutes before turning puddings onto serving plates.

serving suggestion Serve with ice-cream or vanilla custard.

Suitable to freeze.

nutritional count per serving
▶ 7.1g total fat
▶ 4.2g saturated fat
▶ 1045kJ (250 cal)
▶ 43.2g carbohydrate
▶ 3.8g protein
▶ 1.2g fibre

caramel mud cake

PREP + COOK TIME 2½ HOURS (+ COOLING) **SERVES** 12

180g (5½ ounces) white chocolate, chopped finely

60g (2 ounces) unsalted butter, chopped finely

5 eggs, separated

2 teaspoons vanilla extract

½ cup (60g) ground almonds

¼ cup (35g) self-raising flour

⅓ cup (75g) firmly packed dark brown sugar

CARAMEL ICING

60g (2 ounces) unsalted butter, chopped

½ cup (110g) firmly packed dark brown sugar

½ cup (125ml) milk

⅔ cup (110g) icing (confectioners') sugar

1 Grease a 2-litre (8-cup) pudding steamer; line base with baking paper.
2 Combine chocolate and butter in a medium saucepan; stir over low heat until smooth. Remove from heat; cool for 10 minutes. Stir egg yolks and extract, then ground almonds and sifted flour into chocolate mixture.
3 Beat egg whites in a small bowl with an electric mixer until soft peaks form; add sugar and beat until sugar dissolves. Fold egg white mixture into chocolate mixture in two batches. Spoon mixture into the pudding steamer.
4 Place steamer, without lid, in a 4.5-litre (18-cup) slow cooker with enough boiling water to come halfway up side of steamer. Cook, covered, on high, for about 2 hours or until firm.
5 Remove cake from the cooker. Immediately turn onto a baking-paper-lined wire rack; cool cake completely.
6 Make caramel icing. Spread cake with icing.

CARAMEL ICING Melt butter in a small saucepan over medium heat. Add brown sugar and milk; cook, stirring, over medium heat until sugar dissolves. Bring to the boil. Reduce heat; simmer for 1 minute. Remove from heat. Whisk in sifted icing sugar until smooth.

Suitable to freeze at the end of step 6.

nutritional count per serving
- 18.7g total fat
- 4g saturated fat
- 1353kJ (323 cal)
- 34.6g carbohydrate
- 5.2g protein
- 0.6g fibre

test kitchen tips

Canned caramel filling is found in the baking aisle in supermarkets. Leftover rice pudding will keep refrigerated for up to 1 week.

PUDDINGS

Italian arborio rice from supermarkets will hold its shape better than locally grown arborio. Any sweet sherry is fine, however one of the nicest is Pedro Ximénez, a sweet dark sherry with a rich raisin-y taste.

spanish caramel rice pudding

PREP + COOK TIME 2¾ HOURS SERVES 8

30g (1 ounce) butter
1¾ cups (350g) italian arborio rice
2 litres (8 cups) milk
2 cups (500ml) water
2 cinnamon sticks
1 vanilla bean, split, seeds scraped
2 x 380g (12-ounce) cans caramel filling
½ cup (80g) sultanas
1 cup (250ml) sweet sherry
1 teaspoon finely grated orange rind
¾ cup (100g) flaked almonds, toasted

1 Melt butter in a large saucepan over medium heat. Add rice; stir 2 minutes to coat well. Stir in milk, the water, cinnamon, vanilla bean and seeds; bring mixture to the boil.

2 Meanwhile, spoon caramel into a 4.5-litre (18-cup) slow cooker; whisk until smooth. Add rice mixture to caramel; whisk well to combine. Cover surface of pudding with baking paper. Cook, covered, on high, for about 2¼ hours, stirring twice during cooking, or until rice is tender and liquid thickened.

3 Meanwhile, combine sultanas and sherry in a small saucepan; bring to a boil. Reduce heat to medium; cook mixture for about 5 minutes or until liquid is reduced by half. Stir in orange rind and set aside until needed.

4 Discard cinnamon stick and vanilla bean. Serve rice pudding warm or chilled, topped with sherry sultana mixture and almonds.

Not suitable to freeze.

nutritional count per serving
▶ 26.3g total fat
▶ 7.3g saturated fat
▶ 2839kJ (678 cal)
▶ 92.7g carbohydrate
▶ 11.9g protein
▶ 1.6g fibre

PUDDINGS

coffee and hazelnut pudding

PREP + COOK TIME 3¼ HOURS SERVES 10

4 eggs

⅔ cup (150g) firmly packed brown sugar

1⅓ cups (160g) ground hazelnuts

½ cup (125ml) pouring cream

¼ cup (15g) espresso coffee granules

⅔ cup (100g) self-raising flour

2 cups (500ml) store-bought vanilla custard

1 Whisk eggs and sugar in a large bowl until combined. Whisk in ground hazelnuts.
2 Place cream in a small saucepan; bring to the boil then remove from heat. Whisk in coffee granules until dissolved. Whisk coffee mixture into hazelnut mixture. Sift flour over hazelnut mixture; stir to combine.
3 Grease a 2-litre (8-cup) pudding steamer. Spoon mixture into steamer. Top with baking paper and foil; secure with kitchen string. Alternatively, cover with a lid.
4 Place pudding steamer in a 4.5-litre (18-cup) slow cooker with enough boiling water to come halfway up side of steamer. Cook, covered, on high, for about 2¾ hours, replenishing with boiling water as necessary to maintain level.
5 Remove pudding from cooker; stand for 10 minutes before turning pudding onto a serving plate. Serve with custard.

Suitable to freeze at the end of step 4.

nutritional count per serving
- 18.2g total fat
- 5.1g saturated fat
- 1350kJ (322 cal)
- 31.6g carbohydrate
- 8.4g protein
- 2.3g fibre

test kitchen tips
To cover pudding, layer a sheet of foil and baking paper together, large enough to cover the top generously. With paper lengthways in front of you, fold a vertical pleat; this will give the pudding space to rise.

STOCKS

fish

PREP + COOK TIME 30 MINUTES
MAKES 2.5 LITRES (10 CUPS)

- 1.5kg (3 pounds) white-fleshed fish bones
- 3 litres (12 cups) water
- 1 medium onion (150g), chopped coarsely
- 2 celery stalks (300g), trimmed, chopped coarsely
- 2 bay leaves
- 1 teaspoon black peppercorns

1 Combine ingredients in a large saucepan; simmer gently, uncovered, for 20 minutes. Strain stock through a fine sieve into a large heatproof bowl; discard solids. If not using immediately, cool slightly, then refrigerate immediately to cool completely. Store, refrigerated, for up to 1 week or freeze for up to 1 month. Bring to the boil before using.

nutritional count per 1 cup (250ml)
- 0.2g total fat
- 1.1g carbohydrate
- 0.1g saturated fat
- 1.9g protein
- 63kJ (15 cal)
- 0.6g fibre

vegetable

PREP + COOK TIME 1¾ HOURS
MAKES 3.5 LITRES (14 CUPS)

- 2 large carrots (360g), chopped coarsely
- 2 large parsnips (700g), chopped coarsely
- 4 medium onions (600g), chopped coarsely
- 10 celery stalks (1.5kg), trimmed chopped coarsely
- 4 bay leaves
- 2 teaspoons black peppercorns
- 6 litres (24 cups) water

1 Combine ingredients in a large saucepan or stockpot; bring to the boil. Reduce heat; simmer, uncovered, for 1½ hours, skimming surface occasionally. Strain stock through a fine sieve into a large heatproof bowl; discard solids. If not using immediately, cool slightly, then refrigerate immediately to cool completely. Store, refrigerated, for up to 1 week or freeze for up to 1 month.

nutritional count per 1 cup (250ml)
- 0.2g total fat
- 5.7g carbohydrate
- 0g saturated fat
- 1.4g protein
- 151kJ (36 cal)
- 2.9g fibre

STOCKS

beef

PREP + COOK TIME 5¼ HOURS
MAKES 3.5 LITRES (14 CUPS)

2kg (4 pounds) meaty beef bones
2 medium brown onions (300g), chopped coarsely
5.5 litres water (22 cups)
2 celery stalks (300g), trimmed, chopped coarsely
2 medium carrots (240g), chopped coarsely
3 bay leaves
2 teaspoons black peppercorns
3 litres water (12 cups), extra

1 Preheat oven to 200°C/400°F.
2 Roast bones about 1 hour or until browned.
3 Transfer bones to a large saucepan or stockpot. Add onion, the water, vegetables, bay leaves and peppercorns; bring to the boil. Reduce heat; simmer, uncovered, for 3 hours, skimming surface occasionally. Add extra water; simmer, uncovered, for 1 hour. Strain stock through a fine sieve into a large heatproof bowl; discard solids. If not using straight away, cool slightly, then refrigerate stock immediately to cool completely. Skim and discard surface fat before using. Store, refrigerated, for up to 1 week or freeze for up to 1 month. Bring to the boil before using.

nutritional count per 1 cup (250ml)
▶ 2g total fat   ▶ 2.3g carbohydrate
▶ 0.9g saturated fat ▶ 8g protein
▶ 259kJ (62 cal)   ▶ 1.1g fibre

chicken

PREP + COOK TIME 2¼ HOURS
MAKES 3.5 LITRES (14 CUPS)

2kg (4 pounds) chicken bones
2 medium onions (300g), chopped coarsely
2 celery stalks (300g), trimmed, chopped coarsely
2 medium carrots (240g), chopped coarsely
3 bay leaves
2 teaspoons black peppercorns
5 litres (20 cups) water

1 Combine ingredients in a large saucepan or stockpot; bring to the boil. Reduce heat; simmer, uncovered, for 2 hours, skimming surface occasionally. Strain stock through a fine sieve into a large heatproof bowl; discard solids. If not using straight away, cool slightly, then refrigerate stock immediately to cool completely. Skim and discard surface fat before using. Store, refrigerated, for up to 1 week or freeze for up to 1 month. Bring to the boil before using.

nutritional count per 1 cup (250ml)
▶ 0.6g total fat   ▶ 2.3g carbohydrate
▶ 0.2g saturated fat ▶ 1.9g protein
▶ 105kJ (25 cal)   ▶ 1.1g fibre

COOKING TECHNIQUES

When cutting a chilli on the diagonal, leave it whole. The seeds are the heat source, so use less chilli if you are intolerant of high heat levels.

To prepare broccolini, trim about 1cm (½ inch) from the ends of the stems, then remove any leaves. Cut in half and use both the stems and florets. Any sprouting yellow flowers are also edible.

To trim beetroot, cut the stems to 2cm (¾ inch) from the bulb, and don't trim the beard at the base of the plant. This stops the colour from bleeding during cooking.

To toast nuts, stir over low heat in a dry frying pan until golden brown; remove nuts immediately from the pan to stop them from burning.

Washing leeks removes any grit or sand from the inside layers. Cut in half lengthwise, stopping at the root. Fan the layers out and wash under fast-running cold water.

To cut a cauliflower into florets, remove the leaves, then cut and remove most of the core. Cut off the florets where they join the centre core. Cut into any size you like by simply cutting through the stem and head of each floret.

To crush garlic, press the unpeeled garlic firmly with the blade of a large knife (top) crushing the clove. Pull off the papery skin and chop the clove finely with the knife. A garlic press (bottom) removes and leaves the skin behind while crushing the garlic.

To use fresh thyme leaves, hold the thick end of the stem with one hand and run the fingers of the other hand down the stem to strip off the leaves. Any small, thin stems that break away with the leaves are fine to use.

COOKING TECHNIQUES

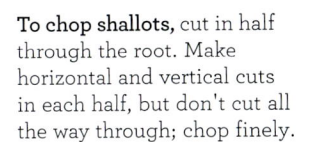

To chop shallots, cut in half through the root. Make horizontal and vertical cuts in each half, but don't cut all the way through; chop finely.

To seed a vanilla pod, cut it in half lengthwise with a sharp knife. Hold the pod and scrape the seeds out with the edge of the knife.

To slice a capsicum, cut the top and bottom off and stand it on one end; slice down removing all the flesh. Remove and discard the seeds and membranes, then slice the flesh.

Chiffonade is a way of cutting green leaves into long, thin strips. Lay leaves flat on top of each other, then roll up tightly and cut into thin slices.

To tie a loin of pork, use kitchen string and tie the pork at 5cm (2-inch) intervals – this helps to secure the shape of the pork, and any stuffing, if using. Avoid slipping the string into the cuts in the rind.

Toasting sesame seeds brings out their flavour. Place the seeds in a wok or small frying pan and cook over a medium heat, stirring constantly, until the seeds are fragrant and golden, about 3-5 minutes. Remove immediately from wok to prevent them from burning.

To cut an onion into wedges, cut the onion in half lengthways through the root. Remove the papery outer skin. Lie the onion cut-side down and cut the onion lengthways through the root into triangular-shaped wedges. The root holds the wedges together so they don't fall apart.

To crush, grind or blend spices in a mortar and pestle, first place them in the mortar (bowl) then pound vigorously with the pestle until they're as coarse or as fine as needed.

GLOSSARY

ALLSPICE also known as pimento or jamaican pepper; available whole or ground. Tastes like a blend of clove, cinnamon, and nutmeg – all spices.

ALMONDS, GROUND also known as almond meal; nuts are powdered to a coarse flour-like texture.

BACON SLICES also known as bacon rashers; made from cured, smoked pork.

BEANS
cannellini a small white bean similar in appearance and flavour to haricot, great northern and navy beans, all of which can be substituted for the other.
kidney medium-sized red bean, slightly floury in texture yet sweet in flavour.

BEEF
blade taken from the shoulder; isn't as tender as other cuts of beef, so it needs slow-roasting to achieve best results.
brisket a cheaper cut from the belly; can be bought with or without bones as a joint for slow-roasting, or for stewing and casseroling as cubes or mince.
cheeks the cheek muscle of a cow. It's a very tough and lean cut of meat and is most often used for braising or slow cooking to produce a tender result.
chuck from the neck and shoulder of the beef; tends to be chewy but flavourful and inexpensive. A good cut for stewing or braising.
gravy beef also known as beef shin or shank, cut from the lower shin of a cow.
osso buco literally meaning 'bone with a hole', osso buco is cut from the shin of the hind leg. It is also known as knuckle.
sausages seasoned and spiced minced beef mixed with cereal and packed into casings. Also known as snags or bangers.
shank, see gravy beef (above).
short ribs cut from the rib section; are usually larger, more tender and meatier than pork spare ribs.

BEETROOT also known as red beets or beets; firm, round root vegetable.

BICARBONATE OF SODA also known as baking or carb soda; a leavening agent.

BREADCRUMBS, STALE one- or two-day-old bread made into crumbs by grating or processing.

BUK CHOY also known as bok choy, pak choi, chinese white cabbage or chinese chard; has a fresh, mild mustard taste.

CARAWAY a spice with a pungent aroma and a distinctly sweet, but tangy, flavour.

CARDAMOM can be purchased in pod, seed or ground form. Has a distinctive aromatic, sweetly rich flavour.

CARROTS, BABY small, sweet, and sold in bunches with the tops still attached.

CHICKEN
drumsticks leg with skin and bone intact.
thigh cutlets thigh with skin and centre bone intact; sometimes found skinned with bone intact.
thigh fillets thigh with skin and centre bone removed.

CHILLI available in many types and sizes. Use rubber gloves when seeding and chopping fresh chillies as they can burn your skin. Removing membranes and seeds lessens the heat level.
cayenne pepper dried, long, thin-fleshed, extremely hot ground red chilli.
flakes dried, deep-red, dehydrated chilli slices and whole seeds.
long green any unripened chilli.
long red available both fresh and dried; a generic term used for any moderately hot, long (6cm-8cm), thin chilli.
powder can be used as a substitute for fresh chillies (½ teaspoon ground chilli powder to 1 medium chopped fresh chilli).

CHINESE COOKING WINE also known as hao hsing or chinese rice wine; made from fermented rice, wheat, sugar and salt with a 13.5 per cent alcohol content. Found in Asian food shops; if you can't find it, replace with mirin or sherry.

COCOA POWDER also known as cocoa; dried, unsweetened, roasted then ground cocoa beans (cacao seeds).
dutch cocoa is treated with an alkali to neutralize its acids. It has a reddish-brown colour, mild flavour, and is easy to dissolve in liquids.

CORIANDER the leaves, stems and roots of coriander are used in Thai cooking; wash roots well before using. Is also available ground or as seeds; do not substitute these for fresh coriander as the tastes are completely different.

CREAM we use fresh cream, also known as pure cream and pouring cream, unless otherwise stated.

CUMIN also known as zeera or comino; has a spicy, nutty flavour, and is available in seed form or dried and ground.

CURRY LEAVES available fresh or dried and have a mild curry flavour; use like bay leaves.

CURRY PASTES some recipes in this book call for commercially prepared pastes of varying strengths and flavours. Use whichever one you feel best suits your spice-level tolerance.
korma a mix of mostly heat-free spices, forms the base of a mild, almost nutty, slow-cooked curry.
powder a blend of ground spices that include chilli, cinnamon, coriander, mace, fennel, fenugreek, cumin, cardamom and turmeric. Can be mild or hot.
red probably the most popular curry paste; a hot blend of red chilli, garlic, shallot, lemon grass, salt, galangal, shrimp paste, kaffir lime peel, coriander, cumin and paprika.
rogan josh a medium-hot blend that is a specialty of Kashmir in northern India. It features tomatoes, fenugreek, cumin coriander and paprika.
vindaloo a hot and fiery combination of vinegar, tomatoes, chilli and other spices.

EGGPLANT also known as aubergine.
baby also known as finger or japanese eggplant; very small and slender so can be used without disgorging.

FENUGREEK a member of the pea family, the seeds have a bitter taste; the ground seeds are a traditional ingredient in Indian curries, powders and pastes.

FIVE-SPICE POWDER also known as chinese five-spice; a fragrant mixture of ground cinnamon, cloves, star anise, sichuan pepper and fennel seeds.

FLOUR
cornflour also known as cornstarch; used as a thickening agent.
plain all-purpose flour made from wheat.
self-raising plain flour sifted with baking powder in the proportion of 1 cup flour to 2 teaspoons baking powder.

GARAM MASALA a blend of spices including cardamom, cinnamon, cloves, coriander, fennel and cumin, roasted and ground together. Black pepper and chilli can be added for a hotter version.

GHEE a type of clarified butter where the milk solids are cooked until they are a golden brown, which imparts a nutty flavour and sweet aroma; this fat can be heated to a high temperature without burning. Available from many Indian supermarkets. Replace with clarified butter, if you can't find it.

GINGER also known as green or root ginger; the thick root of a tropical plant.

GLOSSARY

ground also known as powdered ginger; cannot be substituted for fresh ginger.
GRAVY POWDER an instant gravy mix made with browned flour. Plain flour can be used instead for thickening. Available from supermarkets in a variety of flavours.
HARISSA a Moroccan sauce or paste that's made from dried chillies, cumin, garlic, oil and caraway seeds. The paste, available in a tube, is extremely hot and should not be used in large amounts; bottled harissa sauce is more mild, but if you're not used to the heat, it can still blow your head off. It's available from Middle-Eastern supermarkets.
HORSERADISH CREAM a paste of grated horseradish, mustard seeds, oil and sugar.
KITCHEN STRING made of a natural product such as cotton or hemp so that it neither affects the flavour of the food it's tied around nor melts when heated.
KUMARA the Polynesian name of an orange-fleshed sweet potato that is often confused with yam.
LAMB
forequarter chops from the shoulder end of the lamb.
shanks, french-trimmed also known as drumsticks or frenched shanks; the gristle and narrow end of the bone is discarded and the meat is trimmed.
shoulder from the shoulder. Is very hard to carve with the bone in; to make carving easier, butchers will bone it and sell it as a boneless rolled shoulder.
LEEK a member of the onion family; looks like a giant green onion but is more subtle and mild in flavour.
baby, or pencil leeks, are essentially young, slender leeks; available early in the season, they can be cooked and eaten like asparagus.
LENTILS (red, brown, yellow) dried pulses identified by and named after their colour.
green lentils (australian green lentils) These French green lentils are a local cousin to the famous (and very expensive) French lentils du puy; these green-blue, tiny lentils have a nutty, earthy flavour and a hardy nature that allows them to be rapidly cooked without disintegrating.
MARSALA a sweet, fortified wine to which additional alcohol has been added, most commonly in the form of brandy.

MINCE also known as ground meat.
MOROCCAN SEASONING available from most Middle-Eastern food stores, spice shops and major supermarkets. Turmeric, cinnamon and cumin add authentic Moroccan flavouring to dishes.
MUSHROOMS
button small, cultivated white mushrooms with a mild flavour.
portobello mature swiss browns. Large, dark brown mushrooms with full-bodied flavour; ideal for filling or barbecuing.
shiitake when fresh, are also known as chinese black or forest mushrooms; although cultivated, have the earthiness and taste of wild mushrooms. When dried, they are known as donko or dried chinese mushrooms; rehydrate before use.
swiss brown also known as cremini or roman, light to dark brown mushrooms with full-bodied flavour. Button or cup mushrooms can be substituted for swiss brown mushrooms.
MUSTARD
dijon pale brown, distinctively flavoured, fairly mild-tasting french mustard.
seeds, black also known as brown mustard seeds; they are more pungent than the yellow (or white) seeds that are used in prepared mustards.
wholegrain also known as seeded mustard. A french-style coarse-grain mustard made from crushed mustard seeds and dijon-style french mustard.
OILS
cooking-oil spray we use a cholesterol-free cooking spray made from canola oil.
olive made from ripened olives. Extra virgin and virgin are the best, while extra light or light refers to taste, not fat levels.
peanut pressed from ground peanuts; most commonly used oil in Asian cooking because of its high smoke point (capacity to handle high heat without burning).
sesame made from roasted, crushed, white sesame seeds; a flavouring rather than a cooking medium.
vegetable sourced from plants rather than animal fats.
OLIVES
black have a richer and more mellow flavour than the green ones and are softer in texture. Sold either plain or in a piquant marinade.
green those harvested before fully ripened and are, as a rule, denser and more bitter than their black relatives.

ONIONS
baby also known as pickling onions and cocktail onions; are baby brown onions, though are larger than shallots.
brown and white are interchangeable, however, white onions have a more pungent flesh.
green also known as scallion or, incorrectly, shallot; an immature onion picked before the bulb has formed, it has a long, bright-green edible stalk.
shallots also called french shallots, golden shallots or eschalots; small, brown-skinned, elongated members of the onion family. Grows in tight clusters similar to garlic.
spring have small white bulbs and long, narrow, green-leafed tops.
red also known as spanish, red spanish or bermuda onion; a sweet-flavoured, large, purple-red onion.
PAPRIKA ground, dried, sweet red capsicum (bell pepper); there are many types available, including sweet, hot, mild and smoked.
PARSLEY, FLAT-LEAF also known as continental or italian parsley.
PEPPERCORNS
black picked when the berry is not quite ripe, then dried until it shrivels and the skin turns dark brown/black. It's the strongest flavoured of the three (white, green and black) – slightly hot with a hint of sweetness.
green soft, unripe berry of the pepper plant, usually sold packed in brine (occasionally found dried, packed in salt). Has a distinctive fresh taste.
pink a dried berry from a type of rose plant grown in Madagascar, usually sold packed in brine (occasionally found freeze-dried); they possess a distinctive pungently sweet taste.
sichuan also known as szechuan or chinese pepper, native to the Sichuan province of China. A mildly-hot spice that comes from the prickly ash tree. Although not related to the peppercorn family, its small, red-brown aromatic berries look like black peppercorns and have a distinctive peppery-lemon flavour and aroma. They should always be dry-roasted to bring out the flavour.
white is less pungent; has been allowed to ripen, after which the skin is removed and the berry is dried. The result is a smaller, smoother-skinned, light-tan berry with a milder flavour.

GLOSSARY

PEPPER MEDLEY is a mixture of black, white, green and pink peppercorns, coriander seeds and allspice, sold in disposable grinders in all supermarkets.

PISTACHIOS delicately flavoured green nuts inside hard off-white shells. Available salted or unsalted. We use the weight of shelled nuts in our recipes.

POLENTA also known as cornmeal; a flour-like cereal made of dried corn (maize) sold ground in several different textures. Is also the name of the dish made from it.

PORK
american-style pork spare ribs usually sold in long slabs or racks of 10 to 12 ribs, trimmed so little fat remains; are the ones to slather with barbecue sauce before cooking.
ham hock the lower portion of the leg; includes the meat, fat and bone. Most have been cured, smoked or both, but fresh hocks are sometimes available.
scotch fillet sometimes called neck; a boneless cut from the foreloin.
shoulder joint sold with the bone in or out. Can be bought as smaller cuts or as a whole roasting joint.

POTATOES, BABY NEW also known as chats; not a separate variety but an early harvest with very thin skin; good unpeeled steamed and eaten, hot or cold, in salads.

PRESERVED LEMON RIND a North African specialty; lemons are quartered and preserved in salt and lemon juice or water. To use, remove and discard pulp, squeeze juice from rind, rinse rind well; slice thinly. Sold in delicatessens and major supermarkets.

RAISINS dried sweet grapes.

RICE
basmati a white, fragrant long-grained rice. Wash several times before cooking.
medium-grain previously sold as calrose rice; extremely versatile rice that can be substituted for short- or long-grain rices if necessary.

RISONI small, rice-shaped pasta similar to orzo; used in soups and salads.

SAFFRON available in strands (threads) or ground form; imparts a yellow-orange colour to food once infused. Quality varies greatly; the best is the most expensive spice in the world. Should be stored in the freezer.

SAUCES
char siu a Chinese barbecue sauce made from sugar, water, salt, fermented soya bean paste, honey, soy sauce, malt syrup and spices. Found at most supermarkets.
fish also called nam pla or nuoc nam; made from pulverised salted fermented fish, most often anchovies. Has a very pungent smell and strong taste, so use according to your taste level.
oyster Asian in origin, this rich, brown sauce is made from oysters and their brine, cooked with salt and soy sauce, and thickened with starches.
soy also known as sieu, is made from fermented soya beans. Several variations are available in most supermarkets and Asian food stores. We use a mild Japanese variety in our recipes; possibly the best table soy and the one to choose if you only want one variety.
soy, light a fairly thin, pale but salty tasting sauce; used in dishes in which the natural colour of the ingredients is to be maintained. Not to be confused with salt-reduced or low-sodium soy sauces.
tamari a thick, dark soy sauce made mainly from soya beans without the wheat used in standard soy sauces.
tomato pasta made from a blend of tomatoes, herbs and spices.
worcestershire this dark-coloured condiment is made from garlic, lime, soy sauce, tamarind, onions, molasses, anchovies, vinegar and seasonings.

SAUSAGES minced meat seasoned with salt and spices, mixed with cereal and packed into casings. Also known as snags or bangers.
italian pork a pork sausage often added to pasta sauces. Varieties include sweet Italian sausage, which is flavoured with garlic and fennel seeds; and hot Italian sausage, which has chilli added.

SOUR CREAM a thick commercially-cultured soured cream with a minimum fat content of 35%.

SOURDOUGH around since ancient times, sourdough has a lightly sour taste from the yeast starter culture used to make the bread. A low-risen bread with a dense centre and crisp crust.

SUGAR
caster also known as superfine or finely granulated table sugar.
brown a soft, finely granulated sugar retaining molasses for its characteristic colour and flavour.
dark brown a moist, dark brown sugar with a rich distinctive full flavour coming from natural molasses syrup.
white a coarsely granulated table sugar, also known as crystal sugar.

SULTANAS dried grapes, also known as golden raisins.

TABASCO brand name of an extremely fiery sauce made from vinegar, thai red chillies and salt.

TAMARI see sauces.

TOMATOES
egg also called plum or roma; these are smallish, oval-shaped tomatoes much used in Italian cooking or salads.
paste triple-concentrated tomato puree.
puree canned pureed tomatoes (it is not the same as tomato paste). Substitute with fresh peeled and pureed tomatoes.

TURMERIC, GROUND a member of the ginger family, its root is dried and ground, resulting in the rich yellow powder that gives many Indian dishes their characteristic yellow colour. It is intensely pungent in taste but not hot.

VANILLA EXTRACT made by extracting the flavour from the vanilla bean pod; the pods are soaked, usually in alcohol, to capture the authentic flavour.

VINEGAR
balsamic originally from Modena, Italy, there are now many balsamic vinegars on the market. Made from the juice of Trebbiano grapes; it is a deep rich brown colour with a sweet and sour flavour.
brown malt made from fermented malt and beech shavings.
cider (apple cider) made from crushed fermented apples.
white made from the spirit of cane sugar.
white balsamic is a clear and lighter version of balsamic vinegar; it has a fresh, sweet, clean taste.
white wine made from a blend of white wines.

YOGHURT we use plain yoghurt unless otherwise indicated.
greek-style a full-cream yoghurt often made from sheep milk; its thick, smooth consistency, almost like whipped cream, is attained by draining off the milk liquids.

ZUCCHINI also known as courgette; small green, yellow or white vegetable belonging to the squash family. When harvested young, its edible flowers can be stuffed then deep-fried or oven-baked.

INDEX

A
apricot chicken 15

B
beef
    beef casserole with cheesy herb dumplings 35
    bourbon-glazed beef ribs 36
    chinese braised beef cheeks 40
    coriander beef curry 43
    moroccan beef meatballs 28
    pho bo 24
    pulled beef with barbecue sauce 39
    steak and pepper dumpling pie 26
    stock 111
    tuscan beef stew 31
bourbon-glazed beef ribs 36
bread roll
    pulled beef with barbecue sauce 39

C
cake
    caramel mud cake 104
cannelloni, spinach and three cheese 88
caramel
    icing 104
    mud cake 104
    rice pudding, spanish 107
casserole, beef, with cheesy herb dumplings 35
cassoulet 56
cauliflower cheese 91
cheese, tomato and olive bread pudding 82
cheesy coleslaw 64
cherry puddings, chocolate and 100
chicken
    apricot chicken 15
    chicken hot and sour soup 8
    chicken mulligatawny 16
    honey-mustard chicken 12
    sticky balsamic roast chicken 20
    stock 111
chinese braised beef cheeks 40
chocolate and cherry puddings 100
coffee and hazelnut pudding 108
coleslaw, cheesy 64
coriander beef curry 43
curry
    coriander bee f 43
    lamb and baby eggplant curry with cashew and coconut 63
    lamb and spinach korma 44
    pork vindaloo 71
    paste, korma 44

D
dumpling(s)
    cheesy herb, with beef casserole 35
    pie, steak and pepper 26

E
eggplant
    chilli and tomato stew with ricotta 99
    olive and pine nut pasta sauce 92

F
fetta, lemon and herb rolled lamb 46
fish stock 110
five-spice caramel pork belly 68

G
greek-style dill and lemon lamb shoulder 52
gremolata 79

H
ham and green lentil soup with gremolata 79
hazelnut pudding, coffee and 108
honey-mustard chicken 12

I
icing, caramel 104

K
korma curry paste 44

L
lamb
    cassoulet 56
    fetta, lemon and herb rolled lamb 46
    greek-style dill and lemon lamb shoulder 52
    lamb and baby eggplant curry with cashew and coconut 63
    lamb and rosemary stew 51
    lamb and spinach korma curry 44
    lamb with sage and prosciutto 55
    lamb, spinach and chickpea rice pilaf 48
    lancashire hot pot 60
    turkish lamb shawarma 59

INDEX

lancashire hot pot 60
lasagne, pumpkin, sage and zucchini 96

M
meatballs, moroccan beef 28
moroccan beef meatballs 28
mulligatawny, chicken 16

P
parmesan and spinach bean ragù 84
pasta
    pasta sauce, eggplant, olive and pine nut 92
    pumpkin, sage and zucchini lasagne 96
    spinach and three cheese cannelloni 88
peking duck 19
pho bo 24
pilaf, lamb, spinach and chickpea rice 48
plum puddings, sago 102
pork
    five-spice caramel pork belly 68
    ham and green lentil soup with gremolata 79
    pork and chilli stew 72
    pork vindaloo 71
    pork with prunes 66
    smoky sticky pork ribs with coleslaw 64
    spanish cocido 75
    sweet and sour italian pork with capsicum 76
portuguese turkey 10
poultry
    apricot chicken 15
    chicken hot and sour soup 8
    chicken mulligatawny 16
    honey-mustard chicken 12
    peking duck 19
    portuguese turkey 10
    sticky balsamic roast chicken 20
    turkey with bacon, celery and sage seasoning 22
puddings
    chocolate and cherry puddings 100
    sago plum puddings 102
    caramel mud cake 104
    spanish caramel rice pudding 107
    coffee and hazelnut pudding 108
pulled beef with barbecue sauce 39
pumpkin, sage and zucchini lasagne 96

R
ragù, parmesan and spinach bean 84
ribs
    bourbon-glazed beef 36
    smoky sticky pork ribs with coleslaw 64
rice pilaf, lamb, spinach and chickpea 48
rolls & wraps
    pulled beef with barbecue sauce 39
    turkish lamb shawarma 59

S
smoky chickpea and tomato soup 95
smoky sticky pork ribs with coleslaw 64
soup
    chicken hot and sour 8
    chicken mulligatawny 16
    ham and green lentil soup with gremolata 79
    smoky chickpea and tomato 95
    vegetable harira 87
spanish caramel rice pudding 107
spanish cocido 75
spinach and three cheese cannelloni 88
steak and pepper dumpling pie 26
stew
    eggplant, chilli and tomato with ricotta 99
    lamb and rosemary 51
    pork and chilli stew 72
    spanish cocido 75
    tuscan beef 31
sticky balsamic roast chicken 20
stocks
    beef 111
    chicken 111
    fish 110
    vegetable 110
stuffed capsicums 80
sweet and sour italian pork with capsicum 76

T
tomato and smoky chickpea soup 95
turkey
    portuguese 10
    with bacon, celery and sage seasoning 22
turkish lamb shawarma 59
tuscan beef stew 31

V
veal
    with marsala and mushrooms 32
vegetable harira 87
vegetable stock 110
vegetables
    cauliflower cheese 91
    cheese, tomato and olive bread pudding 82
    eggplant, chilli and tomato stew with ricotta 99
    eggplant, olive and pine nut pasta sauce 92
    parmesan and spinach bean ragù 84
    pumpkin, sage and zucchini lasagne 96
    smoky chickpea and tomato soup 95
    spinach and three cheese cannelloni 88
    stock 110
    stuffed capsicums 80
    vegetable harira 87

W
wraps & rolls
    pulled beef with barbecue sauce 39
    turkish lamb shawarma 59

Published in 2013 by Bauer Media Books, Sydney
Bauer Media Books is a division of Bauer Media Limited.

BAUER MEDIA GROUP

BAUER MEDIA BOOKS
Publishing director Gerry Reynolds
Publisher Sally Wright
Director of sales, marketing & rights Brian Cearnes
Editorial & food director Pamela Clark
Creative director & designer Hieu Chi Nguyen
Art director Hannah Blackmore
Senior editor Wendy Bryant
Food editor Sophia Young
Special sales manager Simone Aquilina
Marketing manager Bridget Cody
Senior business analyst Rebecca Varela
Operations manager David Scotto
Production manager Corinne Whitsun-Jones
Circulation manager Nicole Pearson
Demand forecast analyst Rebecca Williams
Published by Bauer Media Books, a division of Bauer Media Ltd, 54 Park St, Sydney;
GPO Box 4088, Sydney, NSW 2001.
phone (02) 9282 8618; fax (02) 9126 3702.

Printed by Toppan Printing Co, China.

Australia Distributed by Network Services,
phone +61 2 9282 8777; fax +61 2 9264 3278;
networkweb@networkservicescompany.com.au
New Zealand Distributed by Netlink Distribution Company,
phone (64 9) 366 9966; ask@ndc.co.nz
South Africa Distributed by PSD Promotions,
phone (27 11) 392 6065/6/7; fax (27 11) 392 6079/80;
orders@psdprom.co.za

Author: Clark, Pamela.
Title: Slow cooker 3 / Pamela Clark.
ISBN: 978 174245 350 7 (pbk.)
Notes: Includes index.
Subjects: Electric cooking, Slow.
Dewey Number: 641.5884

© Bauer Media Ltd 2013
ABN 18 053 273 546
This publication is copyright. No part of it may be reproduced or transmitted in any form without the written permission of the publishers.

Recipe development Nicole Dicker, Elizabeth Macri, Lucy Nunes, Alexandra Elliott
Photographer Ian Wallace
Stylist Louise Pickford
Food preparation Olivia Andrews; Rebecca Kirk
Cover Greek-style dill and lemon lamb shoulder, page 52

To order books
phone 136 116 (within Australia) or
order online at www.awwcookbooks.com.au
Send recipe enquiries to:
recipeenquiries@bauer-media.com.au

Receive your much-loved Women's Weekly Cookbooks delivered to your door each month

SAVE OVER $55*

Subscribe to the AWW iconic cookbook collection

Your offer choices:

- **Subscribe for 6 months for only $59.95 SAVING $17.75 (23%).** Receive one cookbook every month for 6 months.

- **Subscribe for 12 months for only $99.95 SAVING $55.45 (36%).** Receive one cookbook every month for 12 months.

www.magshop.com.au/cookbooksub1
136 116 and quote M1206BKS

For Terms & Conditions, visit www.magshop.com.au/cookbooksub1. If you do not want your information provided to any organisation not associated with this promotion, please indicate this clearly at the time of subscription. Offer valid until 31.12.2013 to Australian residents only. Prices & savings based on RRP of each book at $12.95. Allow 4-6 weeks for your first cookbook to arrive. One cookbook per month will be delivered by Australia Post (either 6 or 12 – depending on the subscription ordered). Cookbooks will be dispatched before 15th of each month. Cover images of cookbooks are subject to change and covers shown on this page are not necessarily part of the subscription offer. *$55.45 saving is based on a paid 12 book subscription.